THE WALTER LYNWOOD FLEMING
LECTURES IN SOUTHERN HISTORY

D1258309

THE INDIANS' NEW SOUTH

THE INDIANS' NEW SOUTH

CULTURAL CHANGE IN THE
COLONIAL SOUTHEAST

JAMES AXTELL

LOUISIANA STATE UNIVERSITY PRESS
BATON ROUGE AND LONDON

Copyright © 1997 by James Axtell
All rights reserved
Manufactured in the United States of America
First printing
06 05 04 03 02 01 00 99 98 97   5 4 3 2 1

Designer: Rebecca Lloyd Lemna
Typeface: 10.5 on 13 Galliard
Typesetter: Impressions Book and Journal Services, Inc.
Printer and Binder: Thomson-Shore, Inc.

Library of Congress Cataloging-in-Publication Data

Axtell, James.
    The Indians' new south : cultural change in the colonial southeast
/ James Axtell.
        p.   cm. — (The Walter Lynwood Fleming lectures in southern
history)
    Includes index.
    ISBN 0-8071-2171-1 (alk. paper). —ISBN 0-8071-2172-X (pbk. :
alk. paper)
    1. Indians of North America—Southern States—History.   2. Indians
of North America—Southern States—Social conditions.   3. Indians of
North America—Southern States—Government relations.   4. Spain—
Colonies—America.   5. America—Discovery and exploration—Spanish.
I. Title.   II. Series.
E78.S65A97   1997
975'.02—dc21   96-39945
                                                                    CIP

FOR SUSAN

CONTENTS

ILLUSTRATIONS

ACKNOWLEDGMENTS

WHEN I was asked to deliver the fifty-eighth series of Walter Lynwood Fleming Lectures in Southern History, I was at once delighted and nonplussed. No historian could be anything but honored by an invitation to talk in the series that is not only the touchstone and standard in the history of the South but one of the oldest and most venerated in the profession. But I was also somewhat worried because I was asked to follow a very long line of distinguished predecessors who had made their names in southern history and because so few of them were colonial historians, perhaps three or four, depending on how or whom you count. Not only did the vast majority of them focus on the nineteenth-century South, with the Civil War at its heart, but none of them had treated the Indians as lead, or even supporting, actors in southern history.

My anxiety only grew because I have never considered myself exclusively or even mainly a "southern historian." Despite our eighteen years in Virginia, I've always thought of my professional self as a historian of "colonial North America," with a primary focus east of the Mississippi, not south of the Mason-Dixon Line. But then I remembered two saving facts (if rationalization leads to salvation). First, despite the absence of titles with *South* or *southern* in them on my c.v., my research, especially in the past fifteen years, and my teaching always have paid lots of attention to the Southeast and its polychromatic inhabitants. And second, though I was raised in upstate New York and taught to celebrate (if that is the right word for a passel of fallen monks, horse thieves, and regicides) my English and New English ancestors, I had stumbled on a parallel southern ancestry several years ago while looking for something else in colonial South Carolina. If Landgrave Lady Axtell is not enough to earn me at least honorary status as a "southern" historian, I have nothing else to offer, except contemporary residence in the Old Dominion.

Fortunately, none of these tergiversations seems to have bothered the history department at Louisiana State University, who chose me for this signal honor. I am extremely grateful to them and to chairpersons Paul Paskoff and Anne Loveland for enabling me to earn my bona fides, however small, as a southern historian and for their gracious hospitality and good company during my visit in April 1996. I was much taken with the southern charms of the LSU campus, including its Indian mounds and live tiger mascot, and of Red Stick, about which I have read so often in the journals of Iberville, Pénicaut, and Father Du Ru. I owe Paul Hoffman a particular debt for serving as genial tour guide of Natchez (the town and mounded Indian site) and of Cajun cuisine *avec musique*. He, and fellow long-time friends David Weber, Bill Taylor, and Tim Breen, kindly but firmly applied their red pencils to the manuscript when it needed them most. Thanks, too, to the affable and efficient staff of the Earl G. Swem Library at William and Mary, particularly the folks in Interlibrary Loans who good-naturedly honor my requests for odd prints hither and yon.

Maureen Hewitt and John Easterly, my editors at LSU Press, not only attended the lectures faithfully but added enthusiasm to editorial skill in producing this little book. I appreciate their high standards almost as much as their tolerance of an author keen to meddle in book design.

Finally, to my wife Susan, my amusing and bemused muse, goes my profoundest thanks of all. Day in and out, with high tolerance, quiet faith, and consummate grace, she allows me to chase my bookish fancies and fantasies. She is my ideal reader, in every sense. My dedication is small return for hers.

THE INDIANS' NEW SOUTH

Selected Southeastern Tribes at First Contact with Europeans,
1492–1792

THE FIRST SOUTHERNERS

"IN the beginning all the World was *America*," wrote John Locke, referring to the hypothetical state of nature created when Adam and Eve made their social and economic debut.[1] But for us it is more important to remember that in the beginning, all of America was Indian. The human history of America—we should not have to argue any longer—began when Asian hunters first crossed the Bering land bridge 15,000, perhaps 25,000, possibly 50,000 years ago to make the Americas their permanent if peripatetic home. Twelve or fourteen thousand years ago these peoples began filtering into the southeastern regions of North America in search of big game and livelihood, and finding both, they stayed. The great majority of Americans ever since have been Indian, as have the vast majority of American centuries.

These familiar facts should come as no surprise to anyone educated in American schools or re-educated by PBS since 1960. Even our textbooks give them credence in the now-obligatory opening chapter that jets stratospherically over the Indians' long past from arctic Alaska to tropical Guanahaní. But what do these simple facts really mean for American history? Or perhaps more to the point, what *should* they mean? The Indians' exceedingly long tenure on American soil—at least the last thousand of it as semipermanent farmers—suggests that they should be regarded not merely as the first "foreigners" in a long line of "immigrants" who were admitted through the grace and gates of some sort of boreal Ellis Island. Rather, they should be seen by all recent immigrants, from Columbus to the latest boat people, as the original Americans, who settled the continent and staked their claims to it with physical and moral priority, by eminent domain over its flora and fauna rather than by trespass upon any other human possessions. These aboriginal rights call not only for ready recognition in law and morality—the most important goal—but for more extensive, more precise justice from historians, who prepare much of the ground for our collective moral understanding.

Although native rights to America were established in customary fact if not in statutory law early and firmly, we should not assume that the Indian past constituted a timeless or static *"pre*-history" until literate Europeans arrived to pull the natives into the "real" history of identifiable movers and shakers. Indian societies and cultures, we know from archaeology and other nonmanuscript disciplines, constantly evolved and replaced one another, often slowly, sometimes precipitously, while interacting with, adapting to, and being dominated by the powerful forces of nature. In those distant, hard-to-reach societies, as in our own, change was the norm, not the exception, even if its pace was not our frantic own. The appearance of the atlatl (spear-thrower), cultivated corn, paramount chiefdoms, and masked curing societies, whether independently invented or borrowed from friends or enemies, affected the quality of native life as profoundly if not as quickly as the atom bomb, antibiotics, jet propulsion, and televangelists have altered the tenor and course of twentieth-century America.

The numerous advent of Europeans and reluctant Africans after Columbus obviously accelerated the pace of change in Indian America; this is the story in which most of us are interested and the subject of these chapters. But we should also remember that the more focused snapshots of native culture we begin to get at first contact with literate and artistic Europeans freeze the fluidity of cultural time in momentary and misleading stillness, which we must not regard as a necessarily representative or encompassing picture of the larger and longer history of Indian America. It is always tempting for historians to restrict their research to written and published documents easily available in air-conditioned libraries or online; the abundance and richness of written documents doubles the temptation and makes a virtue of necessity. But the fugitive history of native America, before and after contact with Europeans, requires of its students the energetic pursuit and use of documents far beyond the written. We cannot afford to privilege one kind of source over another: We need them all if we are to compensate for—when we cannot recover—the evanescent words and gestures that constituted much of the public past of those oral cultures and face-to-face societies. Thus every student of Indian America needs the special documentation and historical perspective of anthropology, archaeology, linguistics, demography, geography, cartography, art, economics, folklore, and religion, as well as several of the natural sciences upon which archaeologists must draw.

We should also remember that the very act of observing and recording America's native cultures by Europeans subtly and sometimes powerfully altered those cultures, just as a biological specimen is affected by being segregated from its larger environment, squeezed between glass slides, and floodlit under a microscopic beam. The mere presence of a European observer, whether a trader pursuing pelts or a missionary seeking souls, could not fail to alter the behavior and thinking of his native hosts. Likewise, no observer—outsider or insider—possesses an "innocent eye," free from myopia or astigmatism. The objectivity the foreigner may gain from cultural distance he often loses in self-interested pursuits and power plays. It is all but impossible to be disinterested toward a person you are trying to persuade, intimidate, or cajole—or whose aggressive attentions you are trying to deflect.

Despite the misleadingly generic name applied to America's "Indians," native American societies were never identical, seldom allied, and almost never unanimous in their resistance to intrusive Europeans. Because of differences in language, size, environment, history, and goals, they were irremediably factionalized, with virtually no hope of uniting even briefly to repel perceived invasions by the white strangers. The tribes (if we may use that imprecise word) all had different needs and agendas, problems and policies, often articulated in deep distrust of their ethnic brethren and neighbors. Many natives felt no initial threat from the bearded newcomers but welcomed them tentatively, until they could assess the strangers' spiritual and physical power, get what they could from them, and incorporate them into their own polities and kin networks, or reject them as dangerous and malevolent aliens. Like the European invaders, the natives interpreted the new "others" according to preconceived images and conceits, incorporating them into existing historical plots that did not necessarily view the strangers as "gods" nor their advent as particularly auspicious or even noteworthy events.[2]

Whatever the native response, the arrival of people and products from Europe and Africa created a "New World" for the Indians every bit as novel and challenging as the one the European and African immigrants found among the Indians. This world, like its monochromatic predecessor, constantly changed, but it did so at a quicker pace, raising new challenges and higher stakes for succeeding generations of Indian people. If we regard the end of the eighteenth century arbitrarily as the conclusion of one relatively short period in native American history, we should again be aware that we freeze-frame the flow of human time and action and risk forgetting that Indian American history continued, continues, and undoubtedly will continue into the foreseeable future. By virtue of their own cultural conditioning, historians of white America are predisposed to recognize and concentrate on change rather than persistence in the past, and we, too, will register plenty of social and cultural change in the colonial Southeast. But we will also discover surprising continuities in native life that we might be unlikely to seek or find in contemporaneous Euro-American culture.

I seek to show in these chapters that while its native population shrank and its native cultures changed in many remarkable ways in the three hundred years between 1492 and 1792, both the natives themselves and the colonial Southeast remained unmistakably "Indian" throughout. While acculturation, direct and indirect, might alter the appearance, material culture, work, and worship of the southeastern Indians, it could not and did not erase their distinctive ethnic identities as Creeks, Choctaws, and Cherokees, Alabamas, Tunicas, and Apalachees. No one seeking faithfully and fully to portray the region as late as Independence and early nationhood could ignore its Indian peoples, places, or flavor, nor should we.

I

THE SPANISH INCURSION

WHEN Spanish adventurers made their way into the Southeast after 1513, they entered a native world at once promisingly strange and dangerously familiar. The earliest explorers who sailed north out of the decreasingly profitable Caribbean discovered native societies resembling the pugnacious chiefdoms of Hispaniola and Puerto Rico and not the less organized, more biddable villagers of the Bahamas. This discovery was dismaying because the Caribbean chiefdoms, situated in tropical, often mountainous terrain and led by astute and powerful *caciques,* foiled Spanish grabs for power and gold longer and more effectively than would the more populous Aztecs and Incas, at a punishing cost in Spanish blood and treasure.[1] Likewise, the conquistadors who came later, flushed with success and wealth from Mexico or Peru, were disappointed not to find the large, complex, hierarchical, urbanized populations they had conquered relatively easily at Tenochtitlan and Cajamarca. Nor did either group of invaders find the veins or stores of precious metals that made their previous conquests so profitable. But native rumors, wishful thinking, and obliging geographical theories that planted gold and silver in tropical and semitropical zones—wherever the Spanish happened to land—kept the search alive, even in the face of daunting native opposition and unremitting emptyhandedness. Before an official change of plans in the 1560s, their quixotic search for treasure led the Spanish into a native quagmire and a series of deadly and costly failures.

The native societies and polities of the Southeast were well configured to frustrate if not halt the Spanish irruption. Aided by environments and climates inhospitable to the invaders from the dry tablelands and cordilleras of central, western, and southern Spain, the southeastern Indians were organized largely into chiefdoms ruled by chiefs and paramount chiefs whose political power was enhanced by the religious reverence of their subjects. Thanks to the advent of maize horticulture from Mesoamerica after 900 A.D., the southeastern populations had grown appreciably, as had the concentration of settlements around the fields that produced food surpluses for the first time. With the surge in population came specialized divisions of labor, ascribed rather than earned social ranking, and intergroup warfare for political prestige and control of the best farmlands along rivers.

Also from the west came religious cults that exalted political leaders and priests and elevated their houses to the top of earthen platform mounds or around large ceremonial plazas. When these leaders died, they were buried in elite charnel houses or in mounds with elaborate grave goods and sometimes with a number of sacrificed wives and servants to accompany their souls to the land of the dead. In life they were equally distinguishable by their rich wardrobes, transportation on shaded litters, and possession of cult objects such as copper axes, wooden bird effigies with gemstone eyes, or carved shell gorgets in coiled rattlesnake motifs.

The southeastern chiefdoms, which comprised what is known as the Mississippian cultural tradition from *ca.* 1000 to *ca.* 1700 A.D., posed major military problems for invaders because they were essentially alliances of tribal provinces under chiefs who ruled independently or who owed material tribute and military assistance to paramount chiefs. Virtually every village, province, and chiefdom was on a war footing. In societies where every hunter was a well-trained warrior, formidable armies could be quickly mobilized, in small numbers or large, for ambush or conquest warfare. For invading Spanish *entradas* dependent on native food supplies, the ample buffer zones between chiefdoms represented deserts of starvation. The palisades, ditches, and moats around the largest towns, which contained between 200 and 500 houses, proved equally difficult to cross.

Yet, as the Spanish soon discovered, native chiefdoms such as Coosa, Calusa, and Cofitachequi were fundamentally unstable. Tributary provinces jockeyed for position within the chiefdom or strove to break away, either to fashion their own chiefdom or to join another that allowed more autonomy and exacted less tribute. Natural disasters, lost battles, or the death of key leaders could easily cause succession or other political crises. Successful raids and battles upset the delicate balance of prestige and power by capturing numbers of women and children as servants and field hands, destroying temples, charnel houses, and elite lodgings, and desecrating sacred objects, including the corpses of high-ranking ancestors with whom the defeated or retreating leaders felt close kinship.[2]

The earliest Spanish invaders, of course, were ignorant of these obstacles, and later ones seem not to have learned much if anything from the hard experiences of their predecessors. In one sense, the native conditions found in the huge region the Spanish claimed as "La Florida" initially were not a great impediment. Even before Juan Ponce de León put Florida on the European map, unlicensed Spanish entrepreneurs from the Caribbean made their secret way to the peninsula and its keys to pluck Indians from the shore for enslavement in Hispaniola, where the native population was rapidly being depleted by disease, overwork, and cruelty. Some of these victims must have escaped and returned home, perhaps in the company of local Indians also seeking to escape Spanish hands. When Ponce de León explored the west coast of Florida in June 1513, he met an Indian representing cacique Carlos "who understood the Spaniards" and was believed to have come from "La Española, or from another island inhabited by Spaniards." Although Ponce de León purloined a couple of natives to act as guides and future interpreters, his initial goal was only to locate the fabled island of Bimini, which promised riches and perhaps "that celebrated fountain, which the Indians said turned men from old men [into] youths."[3] Other escapees like Carlos's man must have given lively seminars in their coastal villages on the temper of the hairy Castilians they had met and the kind of treatment any Indians could expect if the Spanish should appear on their shores. The attacks and attempted thefts Ponce de León's three ships suffered on both the Atlantic and Gulf coasts may have been instigated by this kind of native intelligence. That Spanish voyages made repeated and large-scale attempts to capture Indian slaves from as far north as South Carolina immediately after Ponce de León's discovery only confirmed the warnings of lucky survivors, of whom there were always too few.[4]

Another group of early Spanish visitors was also largely unconcerned about the size or military prowess of native chiefdoms because they had sheer survival on their minds. After the conquest of Mexico in 1521 and the establishment of regular traffic across the Gulf of Mexico to Hispaniola and through the Keys and Bahama Channel to Spain itself, Spanish ships were frequently caught in storms and driven aground on the Florida coasts. The survivors of these wrecks—largely Spanish but also African slaves, Central American Indians, and native Mexicans—found themselves in the hands of coastal chiefs as slaves and adoptees, and they had much to learn of native locutions, methods, and mores in order to stay alive. Once in rough native hands, castaways found that the relative strength of their captors' polities made little difference to their dire predicament.

Spaniards who brushed the coast briefly or washed ashore as human jetsam obviously had less opportunity to test the full power of southeastern chiefdoms or to alter native culture in major ways than did the gold-seekers who made forays into the interior and the projected colonies that soon followed Ponce de León's discovery and Pedro de Quejo's careful reconnaissance of the Atlantic coast in 1525. Having made a shady fortune in Indian slaves in Santo Domingo, Lucas Vázquez de Ayllón took six ships and 500 Spanish recruits in 1526 to settle a fortified town in a fabled "land of Chicora" near Winyah Bay, South Carolina. With the loss of a large supply ship, the abrupt departure of his Indian interpreters, and the lack of native settlements or fertile farmland to exploit, Ayllón moved the colony south to Sapelo Sound. Within two months, 150 survivors had been driven by disease, mutiny, starvation, rebellious black slaves, and angered Indians back to the Antilles. After their harrowing experience in La Florida, they should have been able to empathize with the 60 South Carolina natives who were inveigled aboard two of Ayllón's ships and shanghaied to Santo Domingo five years earlier. One of the ships was lost at sea. "The Indians in the other died shortly afterwards of sorrow and hunger," wrote a contemporary historian of the Indies, "for they would not eat what the Spaniards gave them." Instead, they preferred "dogs, asses and other beasts which they found dead and stinking behind the fence and on the dungheaps." Those who survived these miseries were allocated as slave labor to Spanish households, goldmines, and fields in Hispaniola.[5]

Pánfilo de Narváez, the one-eyed veteran of Cuban conquests, had no better luck in his attempt to colonize Florida in 1528. His

8

entrada of 400 failed to find the habitable embrace of Tampa Bay, got separated from its supply ships, and was constantly misled by native guides away from the populous, well-fed Apalachee towns of the Panhandle until they despaired and retreated to the sea. After killing the last of their horses, 250 survivors crowded aboard five makeshift rafts and set off for Mexico. Only a handful, including the expedition's treasurer and second-in-command, Alvar Núñez Cabeza de Vaca, reached their destination to tell the tale of their misfortunes and painful encounters with the Floridians.[6]

When Cabeza de Vaca reached Spain in 1537, he led people to understand that La Florida, despite his own horrific experiences there, was "the richest country in the world." Similar rumors enabled Hernando de Soto, newly rich from his part in the conquest of Peru, to recruit several hundred conquistadors for an entrada "to conquer, pacify, and populate" the pagan land of La Florida.[7] After four hapless years careering around the Southeast, as far north as Tennessee and North Carolina and across the Mississippi into Arkansas and Texas, Soto's army of 700 Spaniards and black slaves, 220 horses, assorted war dogs, and a proliferating drove of pigs was reduced to 311 human survivors who reached Mexico in a small fleet of jerry-built brigantines. Soto had engaged most of the largest and most powerful chiefdoms in the region, sometimes imposing his will and hungry troops on them, often suffering their guile, arrows, and formidable resistance. He certainly failed to find gold or silver or to reduce the landscape to peace; like Ayllón and Narváez, Soto drew his last breath and presumably lost his soul in native America.

A few more Spanish attempts to find riches or security in the southeastern interior were equally fruitless and ended equally badly before the crown shifted its geopolitical priorities in the 1560s. When French Huguenots under Jean Ribault and René de Laudonnière planted stone pillars of possession, forts, and a small colony in La Florida after 1562, Spain realized that its first obligation was to rid its North American claims of foreign interlopers, to safeguard the routes of its treasure fleets around the Florida peninsula, and coincidentally to bring the local Indian tribes and chiefdoms to acknowledge Spanish sovereignty. This was the large task of Pedro Menéndez de Avilés, commander of Spain's Caribbean fleet and newly created *adelantado* of La Florida. After liquidating the French "heretics" in 1565, Menéndez proceeded to build a garrison town at

St. Augustine, to establish his capital at Santa Elena on Parris Island, South Carolina, to redeem several European captives from the Indians while befriending or cowing many of the coastal tribes, and to sponsor the first Catholic missionaries in native villages, particularly among the Georgia Guales, the Calusas of southwestern Florida, and the Timucuas of northeast Florida.[8] When English Protestants sent by Walter Ralegh planted a fragile colony on Roanoke Island in the 1580s, hoping to establish a secure base from which to launch privateers against the Spanish flotas, or treasure fleets, the Spanish took alarmed note of their presence. Fortunately, English ineptitude as bad as any shown by the conquistadors in Florida, the same hurricanes that sank many Spanish ships and plans, and the threat to England of the great Spanish Armada killed the colony before the Spanish could.[9]

No matter how numerous or powerful the Spanish were, no matter how long they stayed or how far they penetrated into Indian country, native contact with any Spaniards or other Europeans was potentially momentous, capable of altering Indian lives and culture irrevocably and often for the worse. The brevity of slaving voyages to the South Carolina and Georgia barrier islands, for example, did nothing to mitigate the damage they did to the native lives they touched, directly and indirectly. Two expeditions sponsored by Ayllón and partners suggest the magnitude of the losses to native groups. Sometime between 1514 and 1516, Captain Pedro de Salazar took from a South Carolina "Island of Giants" some 500 Indians, who appeared to the Spanish crew much taller than the natives of the Bahamas and Caribbean. Despite their robustness, two-thirds of the captives died at sea, mostly from starvation. Upon landing in Hispaniola, the weak survivors were "tattooed" or branded and divided among the voyage's backers and other buyers, but most of them died before the Spanish could extract enough labor to justify the high prices they paid for them. Their treatment at Spanish hands contrasted sharply with the hospitality and openhandedness they had shown possibly the first white men in their midst.[10] The loss of hundreds of kinsmen must have shredded the social fabric of the relatively small settlements along the coast, seriously endangering their subsistence, defenses, historical memory, and social continuity. For the survivors left behind, the "social death" of relatives and loved ones was not only a deep personal affliction, but served to breed distrust, fear, and hatred of future newcomers, particularly those who came from the sea in strange, giant canoes. Having learned the hard way that Spanish weapons could kill and maim at a distance, they prepared schemes of ambush and what the victims would call "treachery" in order to defend themselves against any future attempts to steal and enslave them.

Unfortunately, the lessons learned by one group did not necessarily get passed to all the others, even along the same coast. In 1521 Captain Quejo and crew spent three weeks making peaceful overtures to a South Carolina river tribe and allegedly, as Quejo later testified in court, "trying to decide whether to take Indians or not." Lulled by appearances, the natives quickly regretted their credulity when the Spanish sailed off with sixty tribesmen for sale in the slave marts of Santo Domingo.[11]

Yet some groups were unambiguously forewarned about the Spanish disregard for native life and liberty. Tribes or villages from which the Spanish kidnapped likely lads they intended to train as guides and interpreters for future expeditions usually got the message without difficulty. If the Indians had second thoughts when the Spanish returned with their sons, who now sported new looks, clothes, names, tongues, and shiny gifts, the young men themselves quickly dispelled them by running away from their captors and stiffening their people's resistance with cautionary tales and horror stories about Hispanic behavior and values. One of the few survivors of Ayllón's slaving voyage of 1521 was a young boy renamed Francisco, who returned to his home on Winyah Bay with Ayllón's colony five years later. Having learned Castilian well, "el Chicorano" (as he was nicknamed) had been educated and converted by Ayllón, taken to Spain, and treated "as if [Ayllón] had procreated him." Having filled his new father's ears with tall tales of the large, excellent pearls in his homeland and gotten him to bankroll an expedition to those parts, Francisco deserted the Spanish within days, never to be seen again by Spaniards but undoubtedly heard by his native kin and neighbors, who helped ensure the demise of the colony with arrows.[12]

In 1570 a young Virginian who had been taken by the Spanish from the York or James River ten years before exacted revenge even more directly when he was returned home to interpret for eight Jesuit missionaries. Although to all appearances he had been thoroughly hispanicized by Menéndez in Mexico City and Havana, sponsored in baptism by the viceroy of New Spain (whose name he took), and presented to the king in Spain, Don Luis de Velasco quickly ran away to his own people, reassumed native dress, took several Indian wives, and led a lethal attack on the mission with hatchets the priests had traded for corn.[13]

Other challenges to and changes in native life also came from the sea, often after pyrotechnical southern storms. As unlikely as it might seem, the flotsam of Spanish shipwrecks was also capable of affecting native culture in often unpredictable ways. The first novelties to wash up were material goods: ship parts, cargo, and the personal belongings of passengers and crew. When Narváez's entrada arrived in Tampa Bay in 1528, they found the local natives in possession of pieces of linen and woolen cloth, shoes, canvas, iron, and "bunches of feathers like those of New Spain," perhaps the beautiful quetzal feather fans or shields that so impressed Albrecht Dürer when he viewed some of Cortés's Aztec booty in Brussels in 1520. More mundane but more significant were several shipping crates "like those used for merchandising in Castile," each of which contained "a dead man covered with painted deerskins." Upon closer inspection the bodies proved to be European, presumably from the wrecked ship. Yet the expedition's Franciscan friars regarded these burial treatments as "some form of idolatry and burned the crates and corpses" to exorcise the evil spirits. This was unfortunate because the natives had obviously treated the dead strangers with high respect: the apparently undesecrated corpses were carefully wrapped in valuable painted skins and consigned to equally valuable wooden containers made with techniques largely unknown to the Floridians.[14]

Salvage of another sort often led Spanish explorers to fatally erroneous conclusions and sent them on wild goose chases. Many ships that foundered off the Florida coasts were laden with gold and silver jewelry and ingots taken from Indian troves in Mexico, Tierra Firme, and Peru. The Floridians eagerly collected these metals from the wrecks, not because they appreciated their monetary value in European terms—they did not—but because of their color, brilliance, and possibly weight and their uses as media for their own artistic forms. Gold jewelry made in naturalistic shapes by the natives of South and Central America apparently was respected by the

Florida natives for its artistic novelty because many pieces were buried unmodified in mounds with their elite owners. Beautiful lizards, jaguars, eagles, scorpions, and human effigies cast in gold may have inspired local Indians to emulate either the shapes or the casting techniques of the artifacts that washed up on their beaches.[15]

The Floridians' reworking of salvaged gold and silver led Spanish conquistadors and sailors to conclude that Florida was a land rich in precious metals, ripe for the picking. Whenever the Spanish landed among coastal Indians, the natives invariably possessed caches of gold and silver rods, beads, pendants, and other forms of jewelry that they had worked by hammering, abrading, drilling, casting, and incising salvaged coins and bullion. Silver rods were routinely cut, drilled, and rounded or melted down and cast into barrel-shaped beads. Silver *reales* were hammered flat, drilled, and incised to make cult effigy pendants worn from the neck exactly like those traditionally made of shell. Thin sheets of gold were cut and rolled into beads for stringing or tinkling cones for fringed clothing.[16]

The Spaniards, of course, fairly salivated over these riches and did their best to wheedle or wangle them from native hands. The trick was to do so without appearing to place too high a value on the metals for fear the Indians would inflate their own modest valuation of them. This was no easy task when common soldiers and sailors realized that some caciques commanded "as much as a million dollars, or over, in bars of silver, in gold, and in articles of jewelry made by the hands of Mexican Indians." Even the caciques of land-poor Ais and Jeaga on the east-central coast of the peninsula were rich from the sea. Spanish prisoners reported that they often saw their captors head for the local beaches after a storm and return with "great wealth, in bars of silver and gold, and bags of reals."[17] When Adelantado Menéndez journeyed in 1566 to the powerful Calusa chiefdom of "King Carlos" on the southwestern coast to redeem shipwreck victims, Carlos gave him a silver bar worth 200 ducats, but Menéndez refused to barter for any more "so that the Indians should not think that he came in search of gold." His men, however, made out like happy bandits, exchanging some 3,500 ducats' worth for what they regarded as "baubles." "For a playing card . . . an ace of diamonds, one [Indian] gave a soldier a piece of gold worth 70 ducats; and for a pair of scissors, half a bar of silver worth 100 ducats." The soldiers got rich so quickly that "they began to gamble," like their new Indian partners "holding the money of little account." To the Indians, the rarity and novelty of a colorful playing card printed on paper and of sharp metal scissors were far more valuable than the shiny metals that they seemed to be able to obtain in abundance with little effort.[18]

Of even greater value to the Indians were the novel humans they salvaged from the surf, who could be enslaved or adopted into their families and households. Since the Spanish flotas contained black Africans and light-skinned Spaniards as well as more familiar brown-skinned Indian people from Central and South America, the Floridians' world view had to expand to incorporate and account for these strangers and the geographies and cultures from which they came. This is never a small undertaking because it involves a major adjustment of a people's ethnocentric sense of uniqueness at the navel of the universe. If it does not reduce their sense of superiority, it certainly complicates it by introducing disturbing intimations of cultural relativism.

While the Indians always had the upper hand, absorbing ship-wreck victims and educating them for useful roles in native society could not happen overnight, particularly with older prisoners. Nor was acculturation a one-way process, for the captives had strongly held ways of speaking and thinking, relating and doing things, that were asserted or at least much in evidence as their captors attempted to replace them with native versions. Some of these cultural habits must have rubbed off on the Indians. We know that Spanish clothes had some cachet in native circles, perhaps more for ceremonial occasions than everyday wear and for the elite than commoners, because they were eagerly salvaged by and divided among coastal tribes.[19]

Language, too, was a valuable item of exchange, especially as the Spanish presence and assertion of sovereignty grew after Menén-dez's appointment. Interpreters who could negotiate in both lan-guages were as useful to the Indians as to the conquistadors. Cacique Carlos even found that a small amount of linguistic accom-modation could turn Spanish captives into more willing tribesmen. Hernando d'Escalante Fontaneda, who had learned four native lan-guages while a prisoner of the Calusas from the age of thirteen to thirty, and a "free negro" interpreter similarly acculturated once persuaded Carlos that new shipwreck victims who simply could not understand their captors' preremptory commands to dance and sing or to climb to the lookout were not unwilling to cooperate and did not deserve to be killed for their "rebellion." Whereupon Carlos told his subjects that "when they should find Christians thus cast away, and seize them, they must require them to do nothing without giving notice, that one might go to them who should understand their language."[20] For one of the most powerful chiefs in all of Florida, this was a noteworthy concession to another culture and a new way to view his suddenly expanding world.

Perhaps the most permanent change in Indian life resulted from the biological amalgamation of the castaways and their native captors. Spanish men and women who found themselves after a time in need of support, companionship, and love married Indian spouses and often produced *mestizo* offspring. So genuine were these attachments that Spanish women, when redeemed by Spanish colonial officials, sometimes elected to return to their native homes, husbands, and children rather than rejoin a Spanish society they had long since ceased to know. Mestizo children not only looked like the products of two increasingly intersecting peoples but often served as mediators and brokers for the two cultures they straddled, a role of great importance as European power made itself felt over wider swaths of the native Southeast.[21]

Although slave raids and shipwrecks were sporadic and unannounced, Spanish entradas into the interior were large, noisy, and soon predictable in their methods. The biggest and baddest was Soto's, which blundered and plundered its way through the Southeast for nearly four years. The effects of Juan Pardo's more focused fort-building expeditions into the mountains of North Carolina and Tennessee between 1566 and 1568 were much more benign.[22] The bloated settlement attempt of Tristán de Luna in 1559–61 simply came unstuck from the beginning and suffered from, more than it hurt, the natives.[23] Yet all Spanish (and French) thrusts into the Southeast bore consequences for its native peoples and cultures. Some changes were temporary and relatively superficial; others were serious and often did permanent damage.

The *modus operandi* of a typical entrada was predicated on obtaining native bearers, guides, and interpreters for the journey, clearing the way of military obstacles, and locating native food to supplement always short supplies, often frustratingly lost at the last moment in American ports to hurricanes, as Ayllón's and Luna's were. After the first, most expeditions brought their own native interpreters, who had been taken on previous voyages and taught Castilian toward their return. Ayllón had Francisco—briefly—and Luna brought a Coosa woman who had been taken to Mexico by Soto's men sixteen years earlier.[24] When Soto's two *lenguas* (literally, tongues) ran off as soon as they were returned home, he was extremely lucky to stumble upon Juan Ortiz, a thirty-year-old survivor of the Narváez debacle who had learned at least two Timucuan languages while in captivity. So relieved was Soto to find Ortiz that he gave him a black velvet suit to cover his tattooed "nakedness," "some good arms and a beautiful horse." After twelve years with the Indians, even this well-bred Sevillan had some difficulty not only with a surfeit of strange clothes but in resurrecting his native language. "He had even forgotten how to pronounce the name of his own country," one soldier recalled, calling Sevilla "Xivilla," and was forced to make a cross with his hand and bow when he could not remember how to announce that he was a Christian to stop the lance of a Spanish horseman. "He was among us more than four days," recalled another, "before he could join one word with another, since upon saying one word in Spanish, he would say another four or five in the language of the Indians, until finally he was again able to speak our language well." He soon proved invaluable as the entrada's mouthpiece. When he died in the late winter of 1542, Soto was forced to use the inexpert services of a young Indian man seized in Cofitachequi two years earlier. "To learn from the Indians what [Ortiz] stated in four words, with the youth the whole day was needed; and most of the time he understood just the opposite of what was asked...."[25]

The elite troops of Spanish entradas were haughty *hidalgos* whose gentle status allowed them to forgo working with their hands, so they invariably brought along a few, mostly African, servants to carry their baggage and do other menial chores. But once ordinary soldiers reached America's native provinces, they, too, felt entitled to lord it over the "pagan" Indians by taking slaves of their own. This desire, coupled with that of the army's general need to transport substantial food supplies, arms, and ammunition, led to Soto's impressment of hundreds of native bearers, or, as they were called in Mexico and Hispaniola, *tamemes,* as he moved from chiefdom to chiefdom.[26] As he came to the head town of each chiefdom, he sought to take the cacique and some of his principal headmen hostage. This was meant to ensure the docility of their warriors and the collection of ample corn and sometimes meat or fish to sustain the army during its uninvited stay and until it could reach the next destination in another chiefdom. Usually the porters were released in the next chiefdom, even though their entry into enemy territory was potentially lethal. At the end of Soto's expedition, many soldiers complained that now-Governor Luis de Moscoso abandoned "five hundred *head* of Indians, male and female" at the mouth of the Mississippi, thinking it "inhuman... in payment of the great service they had performed, to take them away in order to abandon them outside their lands to become captives of others." Many of these tamemes, including boys and girls, had been with the entrada so long that they "spoke and understood Spanish" and had become Christians of some sort.[27]

Because most porters were adult or at least healthy young males, whose martial prowess and knowledge of the landscape made them risky servants, Soto had most of them put in iron collars and chains to prevent escape. Although the southeastern tribes regularly took captives in small numbers from rival chiefdoms to use as slave labor and often cut nerves and tendons in one foot to hobble them, the loss of as many as 400 to 800 males for potentially long periods opened their towns and villages to enemy attack, deprived families of hunting, fishing, trading, craftsmanship, and perhaps planting or harvesting, and truncated the group's social memory and political structure.[28] If hunger overtook the entrada as it moved in an inclement season or through a buffer zone between chiefdoms or a population that hid its food, the native porters suffered the most because they were always fed and covered last and least. In the Soto entrada's final march back to the Mississippi, "almost all the Indians of service died" from exposure, starvation, and disease. Like all armies, Soto's moved on its stomach, quartering for weeks at a time in major towns to recover from punishing reprisals or to wait out winter cold or spring floods. Even a short stay could clean out a town's *barbacoas,* the raised cribs where the chief stored his tributary produce against a public emergency and seed corn for the next planting. "Forced by necessity," the Indians of Aminoya even volunteered to serve Soto's army in hopes that "they might give them some of the ears of maize they had taken from them" on a previous pass through their territory. "Those who came to the town [from hiding] were so weak and enfeebled that they had no flesh on their bones; and many near the town died of pure hunger and weakness."[29]

The Spanish had other needs that required the forced partici- pation of native women, usually thirty or so at a time. Some women, in even larger numbers, were captured to serve as hostages to neutralize their chiefs and warrior husbands. An occasional woman was drafted as a guide or interpreter.[30] And the rival caciques of powerful Pacaha and Casqui tried to outdo each other in offering close relatives to Soto to cement their temporary alliance in mar- riage. The lord of Casqui offered up one of his daughters, "a pretty girl," whereas Pacaha's leader upped the ante by sacrificing one of his wives, "fresh and [allegedly] very virginal," one or two of his sis- ters, "tall of body and plump in figure," and possibly "another prin- cipal Indian woman." Not to be outdone, Casqui later exchanged two women with two Spaniards for a shirt apiece.[31] Whether this kind of female barter was more the result of callous male chauvin- ism or a politic attempt to fend off even worse arrogations by the ruthless Spaniards is hard to tell.

But no one had any doubts about why the larger groups of women were requested with frequency. According to Soto's secre- tary on the expedition, the Spanish wanted the women not only as porters and cooks but in order "to make use of them and for their lewdness and lust," and "they baptized them more for their carnal intercourse than to instruct them in the faith."[32] The entrada's long and short stays in Indian towns clearly led to sexual relations with native women, some of whom complied for gifts, some from a tra- ditional sense of hospitality, and some undoubtedly by force. Just how the natives in general regarded these liaisons is difficult to judge at this distance. If the natives resembled other Eastern Woodland peoples in the next two centuries, they were, initially at least, not racially prejudiced toward the newcomers and may even have been impressed by the spiritual power they seemed to possess by virtue of their advanced technological skills.[33]

They were certainly receptive to Spanish and African deserters who fled the entrada at various junctures, many of whom were enamored of native women they had met while quartered in the women's towns or on the march. En route to Guaxule in the North Carolina mountains, three black slaves were seduced from the march "by the attraction of [Indian] women." Two were persuaded to return, but the third joined forces with the niece of the cacica of Cofitachequi, who also escaped. An eyewitness testified that the couple definitely "held communication as husband and wife" and planned to return to Cofitachequi 250 rough leagues away. Toward the end of the expedition, the "bastard son of a gentleman of Seville" also deserted to the Indians "in fear lest [some of his Spanish colleagues] seize from him as a gaming obligation an Indian woman whom he had as a mistress and whom he took away with him."[34] To judge by their treatment in one of the most powerful chiefdoms, Spanish deserters did not have to fear for their lives. A gentleman soldier from Salamanca and a black slave who slipped away in Ulibahali lived for eleven or twelve years among the Coosans and were still remembered in 1560—eight or nine years after their deaths—when Luna's expedition arrived in Coosa.[35] Presumably, they left behind mestizo and mulatto children, as their fellow invaders and deserters must have done throughout the Southeast in the sixteenth century.

Spanish entradas and European settlements left their mark on native life in three other ways. Largely benign was the gift, theft, or loss of a veritable cornucopia of material objects and artifacts. When Laudonnière and the French twice withdrew from Florida in 1563 and 1564, they purposely left behind a boat and refrained from burning their fort to save its metalware and leftover supplies for their Timucuan allies.[36] Indian porters walked away from Soto's columns with parcels of Spanish clothing and supplies as well as iron chains and collars which they soon filed off and found new uses for. Soto occasionally and Pardo always distributed small gifts to their native hosts and helpers, such as tubular blue Nueva Cadiz beads, hawk's bells, hand mirrors, silver-colored feathers, chisels, knives, wedges, axes, pieces of brightly colored cloth, enameled buttons, leather shoes, and fiber sandals. On his way back to Santa Elena, Pardo even gave some of the coastal chiefs beautifully painted skin mantles and breechclouts that he had obtained from mountain tribes, thereby fostering an intertribal trade that already dealt in such items as Gulf Coast conch shells, which Pardo also gave—perhaps unwittingly—to one important mountain chief.[37]

The impact these goods had on native habits or artistic conventions is hard to assess. Most new materials, such as cloth and metal, were usually given traditional forms and uses. Many objects were monopolized by the native elite and interred with them in mounds or charnal houses. A few European artifacts may have inspired native imitations in local media, as they did increasingly during the next two centuries. In the temple at Cofitachequi, Soto found glass beads and rosaries and Biscayan axes retrieved from Ayllón's ill-fated colony on the South Carolina coast. Some items of skin clothing seemed to have been made by natives after instruction by Ayllón's colonists. Apparently, the Cofitachequans had fashioned "breeches and buskins, and black gaiters with laces of white hide, and with fringes or edging of colored hide, as if they had been made in Spain."[38]

Nearly as widespread but far more malign were the military effects of the Spanish entradas, particularly Soto's. Although they were on foreign and often dangerous ground, the Spanish enjoyed several advantages in motive and materiel. The all-consuming search for precious metals and other instant wealth spurred the Spanish soldiers, from the lowest to the highest, through long and tedious hardships. The Spaniards' pronounced ethnocentrism and assumption of religious superiority, fostered by eight hundred years of reconquest of the Iberian peninsula from the Moors and inflated by unlikely victories over the overwhelming native forces of Mexico and Peru, gave them a leg up on Indians who did not fight for religion or to impose their beliefs and values on others. Even after four years of profitless suffering and losses, Luis Moscoso could rally Soto's tired troops with the old battle cry of the Reconquista, "Come on, men, Santiago, Santiago, and at them!"[39]

Primed with arrogant fervor, the Spanish wielded a large arsenal of offensive weapons. Ships had the capacity—if not always the good fortune—to supply and resupply entradas from the ports of Spain, Mexico, and the Antilles. The novel size and speed of Spanish horses frightened the natives, scattered them in pitched battles, and chased them down on relatively dry ground.[40] If horses could not follow them in bogs and brush, trained war dogs could. No Indian could outrun or escape the jaws of an Irish greyhound or mastiff, and the Spaniards spread even greater fear of the dogs by periodically throwing Indians to them, which led to the coining of a special Spanish word for the atrocity, *aperrear*.[41] Fifteen-foot lances were initially effective in running down Indians on horseback, but the pikes and halberds of foot soldiers quickly proved cumbersome in the southeastern forests, whose warriors seldom attacked head on. More efficient and lethal were crossbows, arquebuses, and particularly double-edged Toledo swords. The Spanish were fierce and expert swordsmen who did not hesitate to slash and hack at exposed native limbs. Twenty percent of the Indian skeletons at the King site in northwest Georgia bore deep gashes and gouges from Soto's swords.[42] At other points along the entrada's route, commoners and caciques alike were slashed in the head and back and had their arms, hands, and noses cut off.[43] When the inhabitants of the large Tascaloosa town of Mabila suddenly attacked Soto's forces in October 1540, the Spanish did not end their revenge until they had killed 2,500 men, women, and children. Not long after, Soto "ordered that no male Indian's life should be spared" when he sicked his troops on Nilco, a town of five or six thousand, in a preemptive strike to terrorize the region.[44]

Because the natives were no match for the well-armed ferocity of Soto's numerous troops and their horses in a showdown, they sought to neutralize the Spanish threat by deflecting, coopting, or avoiding the invaders. At considerable personal risk, Indian guides commandeered by Soto led the entrada away from their chiefdom's major towns and food supplies into barren or enemy territory.[45] If the Spanish wanted to stay put, local caciques allied themselves with the intruders in order to direct Spanish swords against rival provinces and chiefdoms, which invariably upset the delicate balance of Mississippian prestige and power.[46] Having Soto's troops quartered in one's town was a large price to pay, but it was still smaller than being ravaged by angry Spaniards or by a Spanish alliance with a rival chiefdom. And if none of these ploys worked, the Indians simply abandoned their towns and fields to avoid contact, sometimes torching both to deny the invaders any succor or satisfaction.[47] The only place where the Indians could deliver punishing blows to the Spanish was on the Mississippi, where the conquistadors' swords, horses, and heavy armor did them no good and native canoes literally ran circles around the Spaniards' clumsy, exposed brigantines.[48]

Although Soto's entrada made its escape from the Southeast, as did Ayllón's, Narváez's, Luna's, and Pardo's, the unvictorious Spanish bequeathed a legacy of death and disintegration that had little to do with swords or guns. The forces of occupation left behind by every European ship, settlement, and entrada, no matter how briefly they remained in La Florida, were biological. A few were relatively benign. Many of Soto's imported pigs escaped and multiplied prodigiously to become the famous razorback hogs of the southern mast forests, for which many Indian groups acquired a decided taste.[49] Pedro de Quejo's voyage to Winyah Bay in 1525 may have introduced European plants to the native Southeast. According to court testimony, Quejo gave the Indians seeds for various Spanish plants that his employer Ayllón hoped they would cultivate before he planted his proposed colony among them the following year. Even without Quejo's careful instructions in how to grow them, the seeds may have taken on a life of their own.[50]

Certainly other imported plants—and animals—did well in and on the humid soils of the Southeast. Inland natives were often growing peach trees and watermelons before they were contacted directly by Spanish explorers. By the seventeenth century, mission Indians added garbanzos, figs, and hazelnuts to a mixed diet that already included wheat, which was initially grown to make communion wafers for the resident friars. The Indians never took to sheep or goats and only slowly to cattle—the pastoral Spaniards' favorite animals—but carefree chickens and pigs gained instant favor as complements to, if never complete substitutes for, wild game and fish.[51] It is not difficult to imagine the proliferation and hybridization of species throughout Spanish and native Florida of the 600 chickens, 550 pigs, 492 pumpkin squashes, 505 loads of cassava, and 854 *fanegas* of corn that Menéndez imported from Havana in 1566.[52] No one bothered to record the silent arrival of rats and weeds, but they, too, came in the holds of European ships and created a niche for themselves in native fields and villages.

Equally quiet but far more dangerous were those microscopic messengers of death, epidemic diseases. Isolated from the microbial history of Europe, Asia, and Africa by the reflooding of the Bering Strait, America's natives had developed no immunities to serious infectious diseases because they virtually had none.[53] When explorers stepped off ships from the disease capitals of Europe, they brought lethal strains of influenza, typhus, diphtheria, bubonic plague, and smallpox as well as so-called "childhood diseases" such as measles, mumps, and chicken pox. All of these and more throve in the "virgin soil" disease environments of the native Southeast and proceeded to cut down its peoples with merciless efficiency.[54] When Soto's entrada reached the main town of Cofitachequi, over a hundred miles from the South Carolina coast, the Spaniards noticed that several surrounding towns were uninhabited and "choked with vegetation" because the province had suffered a "great pestilence" within the last year or two. Survivors had fled to the woods and planted no crops. In one town the conquistadors found "four long houses full of bodies of those who died from the plague that had raged there." In all likelihood, death had made its slow but steady way, on one human host after another, from Ayllón's squalid colony at Sapelo Sound over the course of ten or eleven years.[55] More rapid was the unfamiliar contagion that felled the seventy-four natives who were laid out at the same time in the Tatham mound in west-central Florida in the wake of Soto's entrada. The presence of only two sword cuts on the skeletons is stark testimony to what must have been the terrifying lethality of the conquerors' invisible allies.[56]

Disease and Soto's destructiveness brought many of the Mississippian chiefdoms to their knees and by the beginning of the seventeenth century had seriously depopulated and decentralized the native Southeast. As the populations of the chiefdoms dropped, often precipitously in the areas visited by Soto, towns were abandoned for lack of viability and their inhabitants moved to less damaged ones, thereby reducing the areal extent of each chiefdom. Most towns, even those replenished with polyglot refugees, covered much less ground than before. Several main towns, particularly in northwest Georgia and eastern Tennessee, moved south into central and southern Alabama, where in the next century they formed the Creek confederacy. Other groups moved into less accessible upland regions between rivers, and those who remained in the valleys built more dispersed, elongated settlements without defensive palisades.

Along with their populations and warrior counts, the political hierarchies of the chiefdoms collapsed. The authority of chiefs declined, as did the ascribed status of the elites, part-time craft specialization, and elaborate funeral rites and differential grave offerings for the elite. Tributary payments and obligations gave way to local autonomy. Paramount chiefs disappeared and tribal chiefs ruled more by persuasion than by force or religious charisma. Mound centers were abandoned and no new mounds were built because chiefs no longer had the coercive power to command labor for large-scale public projects. And the religious cults that had sustained the whole Mississippian hierarchy lost their explanatory power and adherents.[57]

Although the southeastern interior fared poorly, many of the coastal Florida groups retained much of their former strength and belligerence toward the Spanish. Less ravaged by disease because of their dispersed settlements, they successfully resisted Spanish missionaries and attempts to render them obedient to a distant monarch for many decades. Since neither corn nor cattle prospered in the southern two-thirds of the peninsula, particularly along the coasts, the natives held on to their age-old diets of fish and game, traditional lifeways, and familiar forms of government and religion far longer than their Timucua and Apalachee neighbors in the north who allowed Catholic missions into their midst.[58]

Yet for the Southeast as a whole, the Spanish advent offered little redemption; according to some farsighted natives, the foreigners' continued presence promised even less. In 1541, six leaders from an Indian town near the Mississippi visited Soto's camp. "They were come," they said, "to see what people [the Spanish] were" because "they had learned from their ancestors that a white race would inevitably subdue them."[59] Whether the Spanish interpreters or chronicler put words in their mouths or not, the elders' prophecy would certainly *not* come to pass in the Southeast in the sixteenth, seventeenth, *or* eighteenth century. What we will explore in the next two chapters is the very *lack* of inevitability about the European domination of the region and the crucial role the natives played in fashioning their own new South.

THE WIDENING STAIN

NATIVES who came face to face with Soto's numerous and nasty legion can be forgiven for thinking that their world was coming to an end. In one sense, of course, it was: the arrival of Europeans and their bizarre cultural and biological baggage altered irrevocably the isolated world the Indians had known. But the progress of that change for most groups in the Southeast was seldom steady and never fully predictable. With the pullout in 1568 of the small garrisons Juan Pardo left in the mountains of North Carolina and Tennessee, Spanish leverage upon native life for the next century was applied effectively only in northern Florida and along the coasts and barrier islands of Georgia and South Carolina to Port Royal Sound. The removal of the Spanish capital from Santa Elena to the frail but durable presidio of St. Augustine in 1587 shortened even further the invaders' martial reach.

Unable to dominate the natives of La Florida with sword and gun, the Spanish resorted to the colonial weapons that had worked so effectively in their conquests—or, as King Philip II preferred, "pacification"—elsewhere in Spanish America.[1] Catholic missionaries, briefly Jesuits and then Franciscans, sought the Indians' political allegiance while they wrestled shamans and priests for the natives' souls. At a fraction of the economic and moral cost of military conquest, unarmed friars could reduce the natives to at least nominal obedience both to the Prince of Peace and to the king of Spain. In three provinces—Guale, Timucua, and Apalachee—the friars enjoyed considerable success. By 1650, some 26,000 Indians had submitted themselves to the strangers' influence enough to be considered Christian converts. Many of their hereditary leaders were regarded as "*muy españolado*" in dress, language, and deference to their superiors in the Hispanic hierarchy they had accepted as the price of peace, protection, and trade. At all social levels, Florida's mission Indians underwent substantial and often dramatic changes in their individual and communal lives.

Florida's missions might have remained viable and in turn underwritten Spain's ability to safeguard her bullion fleets had the new English colonies of the Southeast not regarded Spanish Florida and its Catholic natives as affronts to true religion and barriers to free enterprise and unbridled expansion. Beginning shortly after the founding of Charles Town in 1670 and climaxing in 1704, English militias and their largely Lower Creek allies destroyed the whole Spanish mission system, thereby launching another round of drastic changes in native life in the Deep South. Indeed, the advent of English settlers, traders, and tradesmen and their African slaves and servants throughout the seventeenth century had induced the natives of the upper and interior Southeast to adjust many of their ways of living and thinking as swiftly and seriously as their counterparts in La Florida had in the previous century. In a native simile, English immigrants, unlike the Spanish, spread over the native landscape "like grease on a blanket," with many of the same results for the owners. Neither the blanket nor the landscape would be the same again.

The first Spanish missions were planted by Jesuits in 1566 among the coastal Guales. But after six years, the blackrobes had managed to baptize only six dying natives, four of them children. The Jesuits' failure had three major causes, only one of their own making. The two outside their control were punishing epidemics in 1569 and 1570, which the Indians not unreasonably blamed on the priests, and the quartering of Spanish troops in mission villages to protect the priests and to enforce social control. The soldiers' appetites for food and women put a severe strain on native hospitality, and the Jesuits suffered as a result. But the Jesuits also gained no ground with the Guales because of their Catholic contempt for the natives' "pagan" rites and "superstitions" and obdurate practice of polygyny and easy divorce.[2]

When the Jesuits abandoned the Florida field in 1572, they were replaced the following year by Franciscans who reoccupied the

Guale villages and moved gradually down the coast and north from St. Augustine into the homeland of the eastern Timucuas in northeastern Florida. By 1607 they counted 6,000 converts in these two provinces. But they had no easier time breaking through the crust of cultural custom than did their predecessors. In 1576 the Guales openly rebelled against the Spanish capital at Santa Elena and in 1597 overthrew the whole missionary enterprise in their region, killing five friars and holding another in rough captivity for nearly ten months. The revolt was sparked by Juanillo (his Spanish moniker), the young heir of the head *mico* of the Guales, when a friar sought to punish him for keeping plural wives by depriving him of his rights of succession. In recruiting allies for his attack, Juanillo made clear the kinds of changes the Guales were asked to make under the missionaries' new regime. "Let us restore our [ancient] liberty of which these friars deprive us," he pleaded.

> We who are called Christians, experience only hindrances and vexations. They take away from us our women, allowing us but one, and that, in perpetuity, forbidding us to exchange them for others. They prohibit us from having our dances, banquets, feasts, celebrations, games and wars, in order that, being deprived of these, we might lose our ancient valor and skill . . . . They persecute our old men, calling them wizards. They are not satisfied with our labor for they hinder us from performing it on certain days . . . . All they do, is to reprimand us, treat us in an injurious manner, oppress us, preach to us and call us bad Christians. They deprive us of every vestige of happiness which our ancestors obtained for us, in exchange for which they hold out the hope of the joys of Heaven. In this deceitful manner, they subject us, holding us bound to their wills. What have we to hope for except to become slaves?[3]

Eight years later, after fierce Spanish reprisals, most of the Guales realized that they would have to coexist with the Spanish and allowed the Franciscans to return. To segregate themselves from their pagan kin and to ensure the purity of the sacraments, Christians moved their villages to the barrier islands along the Georgia coast. About the same time, the friars made their first overtures westward to the Apalachees in the Florida Panhandle. With some 25,000 people and rich farmland, the Apalachee province soon became the focus of Spanish attention, particularly as eastern converts were depleted by disease, defection to the interior, and labor drafts to sustain St. Augustine.

Unlike Guale, the northern interior of Florida came under Spanish influence not by fire but by contracts, ceremonies, and gifts. Caciques from Timucua and Apalachee not only walked to St. Augustine to ask for alliances with the governor, who counted entertainment a far better bargain than war, but invited friars to their villages to install the new religion. The western field was opened in 1608 when the Timucua headman asked two friars to end a three-year war between his twenty-some towns and Apalachee. Accompanied by a troop of Indians shouldering arquebuses and a banner emblazoned with the Holy Cross, a friar typically announced his intentions by throwing down and burning native religious images in the central plaza. This bold act cleared the stage for the building of a standardized Catholic mission and the enrollment of the town in the independent but allied "Republic of Indians," under the Spanish crown.[4]

With only two or three hundred armed Spaniards in all of Florida, Spanish officials had no choice but to try to rule through traditional native leaders and to honor the kinship system through which caciques inherited office. Having learned the hard way in Guale, colonial governors and friars were forced to respect the customary rules of matrilineal kinship, by which native people claimed family lineage and inheritance through the maternal line. This was not easy for the predominantly male colonists from Spain's aggressively patrilineal and patriarchal society. But if the chiefs were to continue to exercise any sway over their people, there was no alternative. Trying to alter the succession (as with Juanillo) or to impose a Spanish puppet in office would only drive many of the tribe northward into the arms of pagan or Protestant enemies.

Not only did the Spanish pragmatically respect the native order of kinship, they supported the authority of the chiefs who showed themselves receptive to Spanish religion and alliance. This support was particularly useful to chiefs caught in factional fights within their councils, often caused by the armed proximity and persistent demands of the Spanish and the less demanding pull of secular traders in the northern interior. Pro-Spanish caciques, some of whom had been raised in style in the governor's house in St. Augustine, also felt free to transfer their higher allegiance away from paramount chiefs and large native alliances to the Spanish king and his deputies in Florida, which drove the final nail in the coffin of the old-style Mississippian chiefdoms. While chiefs occasionally found their authority compromised by captious friars or heavy-handed garrison commanders, native self-government remained the rule throughout the colonial period in Spanish Florida.[5]

To entice and reward the loyalty of native leaders, the Spanish dispensed a liberal array of material goods and legal privileges. As new members of the "Republic of Indians," the counterpart of the "Republic of Spaniards," the natives were guaranteed their sovereignty, their land, and freedom from enslavement. Their legal separation from the Spanish did not deprive them of the protection of their Spanish "fathers" or, what made more sense and was less presumptive in a matrilineal system, their Spanish "cousins." And like hidalgos in medieval Spain, America's native nobles were entitled to the perquisites of rank: horses, swords, ornate clothing, the title "Don," and exemption from corporal punishment, manual labor, and taxation. To reconfirm these rights and honors, the governor or his deputy met annually with each chief to listen to complaints and needs and to distribute an ever-growing pile of gifts: fancies for the *principales*, hats, knives, axes, beads, and cloth for their "vassals," and rich altar furnishings and bells for their new church. Although the chiefs often presented reciprocal gifts to the king, the king's annual and lopsided largesse in St. Augustine led many of them to regard it as a form of "tribute"—their name—to which they were due as the "natural lords" of the country.[6]

Once enrolled as Spanish allies, Timucua and Apalachee chiefs, like their Guale counterparts before them, sponsored the building of Catholic missions and churches in their major towns and chapels in their smaller villages. By definition, the major towns were populous and surrounded, particularly in Apalachee, by productive hamlets and farmsteads. This meant that the new religious order was grafted onto existing settlement patterns, which endowed the chiefs with considerable clout over the friars and the few soldiers who were garrisoned in the major mission towns after 1640. Even the deputy governor stationed in San Luís de Apalachee might find himself recalled if he crossed the Apalachee headman. The only exceptions to the rule of placing missions in existing towns occurred after the

Timucua revolt of 1656. A few former rebel towns were moved south along the "king's highway" between St. Augustine and Apalachee, a smaller number were planted at river crossings to maintain ferries, and some villages were consolidated after depleting raids by northern enemies or English slavers. In some cases, small satellite villages were arranged linearly along trails leading to the mission, rather than in an annular cluster as they were in pre-Spanish times. The Spanish goal was to have loyal villages no more than a day's travel apart along the 250-mile trail.[7]

The major missions, or *doctrinas*, were established in the largest or most prominent communities to ensure that the holy sacraments had a stable, sedentary audience and the exemplary attendance of the chief, his headmen, and their families. Satellite villages, or *visitas*, and farmsteads were served less frequently, partly for lack of priests, partly because a "portable" altar kit consisted of thirty-five items, including a stone altar. The dispersed settlements and seasonal foraging habits of the Indians posed one of the most serious problems for mission officials, who regarded settled homes and fields essential to Indians becoming "people of reason" (*gente de razón*) and therefore capable of being trusted with the sacraments. Until such people could be "reduced" to "civilized"—that is, Mediterranean-style—living, they must remain probationary Christians at best, beyond the Pale at worst. Ideally, members of the "Republic of Indians" ought to live within the sound of the church's bell, some 560 yards according to rules formulated for New Spain. This arrangement not only brought them "beneath the bell of their doctrinas" and the whip "hand of their doctrineros," or priestly instructors, it also gave them substantial "houses and properties to lose" in the event of war or rebellion.[8]

The first Christian modification of a native town was often the substitution of a large wooden cross for the ball game pole that stood in the central plaza of most southern Indian communities. The ball game itself was not particularly objectionable, save for its brutality and the heavy gambling associated with it, but it was surrounded by allegedly pagan, indeed "demonic," preparations and celebrations. As a symbol of the natives' misguided religion, the ball game was the target of a Franciscan campaign, particularly between 1675 and 1684. The head prosecutor, Friar Juan de Paiva, sought its abolition even though its religious role was to bring rain and sun to native crops and the summer intertown contests, which the Creeks called "the younger brother of war," allowed young men to gain honors in peacetime. Other friars and government officials eventually got the ban rescinded by arguing that the game had already been shorn of its offensive pagan rituals and connotations and that it was as deeply woven into the fabric of native life as the practice of consulting shamans for illness, neither of which could be eliminated in a lifetime.[9]

With or without the felling of the ball pole, the erection of a large cross signaled the building of a number of novel structures on or near the town's central plaza. Their novelty came largely from their rectangular shape, because their construction by native workmen incorporated the palmetto thatch roofs and wattle-and-daub walls of native buildings. Native buildings were invariably round with conical roofs, even the *buhío,* or council house, capable of holding as many as 2,000 to 3,000 persons. By contrast, the friars erected squarish structures on a rough grid plan, rather than in a crescent as the natives were wont to do. These buildings consisted of a church (about 60 feet by 35 feet); a *convento,* or residence for the friars; a smaller, open *cocina,* or cookhouse; and occasionally a garrison house for the soldiers sent to protect the priests and their work. Nearby lay the mission cemetery, in whose consecrated ground (*campo santo*) Christian natives were buried.[10] That the Spanish built walls, fences, and palisades around their structures and gardens also must have struck the natives as odd, if not downright unfriendly.[11]

Adjusting their eyes to strangely shaped buildings was nothing compared with the behavioral changes the natives were asked to make by their new fathers. Children and adults alike were put to their ABCs to learn to read and even write their native language and, less frequently, Spanish. This major skill not only gave these oral peoples access to the primers, catechisms, confessionals, and booklets of devotion prepared in the three native languages of Florida, but subtly began to alter their whole consciousness.[12] Perhaps the most momentous effect of literacy is that when the alphabet becomes interiorized, readers can do their thinking alone and no longer need the oral community to achieve consensual meaning. As Father Ong has put it, "The book takes the reader out of the tribe." [13] At a time when native communities were being subjected to a host of centrifugal forces, the introduction of literacy was, unknowingly, a Trojan gift from the invaders.

Once the Indians had memorized a short catechism and a few Latin prayers, they were baptized into a faith that could be enforced like a contract by secular as well as clerical authorities. Having taken on new personae, *los cristianos* assumed new names. Taking the name of a Catholic saint as a personal name—the standard practice—also gave the Indian an acceptable "guardian spirit" to replace traditional sources of spiritual power and guidance. Chiefs commonly took the surname of the reigning governor, who stood as godfather at their christening.[14]

The natives' new allegiance not only earned them the emotional and intellectual solace of a universal religion—which was undoubtedly real and substantial—but entailed upon them a number of duties and restrictions that prevented many traditionalists and apostates from joining them. Christians could not leave their *doctrinas* without permission for fear they would "wander about idly and associate with heathen and fall into . . . apostasy." When the church bell rang seven, in later years four, times a week, they had to drop what they were doing and assemble for indoctrination in the tenets of the faith. They had to attend Mass every Sunday and on feast-days, following a paper calendar they had never known. To spare the friars' eyes, topless women—not a rarity in the Sunshine Colony—had to be decently draped in garments of Spanish moss; as of Bishop Calderón's visit in 1675, there were still 8,162 Christian breasts to be covered.[15]

Macho native warriors, who were encouraged to maintain their prowess and weapons in defense of the Spanish, had to learn to kneel and to confess their shortcomings before overdressed men who had no apparent interest in either war or women. A visitor in 1630 noticed that the sacrament of confession was particularly "insufferable and difficult for the men" and that, at first, they could not kneel properly "because they fell on the ground when they doubled their knees." If this abasement was not enough, they had to cut their long hair "like the Spaniards" and submit their bare backs to be whipped—often by a native *aguacil,* or church assistant—for any of a long catalog of social and sexual transgressions the friars called sins. Although legally exempt, even married women and chiefs, often fingered by native spies, felt the sting of the friar's whip for abortions, concubinage, and adultery as well as for missing Mass. According to the Franciscans as late as 1681, the whip was necessary because "the Indians of Florida want to enjoy freedom to live according to laws of the flesh though professing Christians." The friars' Ten Commandments and Seven Deadly Sins alone constituted a moral minefield for native neophytes seeking social acceptance and spiritual redemption.[16]

For those who tried to play by the new rules, the friars held out the promise of a better—a perfect—life to come. Their earthly reward was to be buried in the mission cemetery or church, separated forever from the mortal remains of their pagan relatives. Even the native nobility were laid to rest prone, on their backs, in simple graves, sometimes in a Spanish-style coffin, always wrapped in a white shroud, perhaps accompanied by a few Christian amulets, headed toward the sacred eastern birthplace of their new religion. By sharp contrast, the souls of those who did not please the Mother Church would, the friars taught, writhe eternally in fires that dwarfed the flaming tortures of their native enemies.[17]

The Church's promise of salvation in the afterlife and its sacramental comforts in the meantime made its strictures and demands bearable for most of the tens of thousands of native converts in the seventeenth century.[18] Far more difficult to stomach was the Spaniards' persistent demand for native labor. As the king's representatives in a garrison colony, Florida's soldiers and friars were supported by the *situado,* a government subsidy that was supposed to be paid annually from the royal coffers in Mexico City. But even when shipwrecks, English pirates, and red tape did not delay the shipment of supplies and salaries, often for years at a time, the situado was never enough to maintain the colonists as Spaniards expected to be maintained. This situation therefore required the services of the local natives in three major forms.

First, when the situado did arrive in St. Augustine, it had to be transported to outlying garrisons and to the missions as far away as Apalachee, usually three times a year. Since the government never supplied Florida with enough horses or mules, Indian porters were pressed into service to do the hauling. Every Christian town had to supply a quota of single men, based on the census of those who took confession—by Church law—every Lent. Each porter was expected to carry 75 pounds of cargo in addition to his own supplies for a

33

round-trip journey of as many as four weeks, though he might receive minimal food and shelter in native towns along the *camino real* and a tiny daily wage in trade goods. If, as Amy Bushnell has estimated, each *doctrinero* annually consumed food and sacramental wine and wax weighing about 1,800 pounds in their containers, the supply of twenty-five western missions required about 10,500 burdener-days a year. To maximize use of the porters, enterprising caciques loaded them on the outbound leg with native products such as bacon, poultry, tobacco, rope, earthenware, and deerskins and friars sent surplus corn and beans, all for sale to the presidio and settlers of St. Augustine.[19]

The Spaniards' second use of native labor was more generalized. Because of the paucity and class-consciousness of Spanish laborers, Indians and African slaves were expected to do the colony's sweat work, such as unloading ships, paddling canoes, cutting firewood, domestic service, and tending the farms and gardens of soldiers and settlers. Another unfortunate group worked on major public projects, such as shipbuilding and the awesome shell-block Castillo de San Marcos, which guarded the capital and its harbor. Eventually, as the native population declined, this kind of labor turned largely into free wage work. But as mandatory *repartimiento* service, it ranked as low on the native scale as cargo-hauling, even though it, too, was generally episodic and (minimally) compensated.[20]

When the Christian Indians were not sweating for Florida's secular officials, they put in time supporting their local padres and improving the church. The heart of the religious labor system was the *sabana,* a field planted in corn, beans, and winter wheat once or twice a year by the whole village for the use of the Church. Often the priests' field produced a surplus, which they sold, along with other products raised on the mission farm, to St. Augustine, Cuba, or Mexico. Native neophytes did all the work at the mission, in and out of the church, and backpacked the saleable produce to the capital or to the Apalachee seaport at San Marcos, all without compensation save the heavenly sort. For as little reward as a knife, those in Apalachee also carried trade goods to northern pagan villages to barter for deerskins, which in turn commanded a nice price in Havana.[21] All of the mission's profits went to feed the friars, maintain and repair the church, and provide "ornaments and things necessary for divine worship," such as candles, wine, altar furnishings, vestments, and bigger and better bells.[22] Many converts were as competitive as their doctrineros in trying to outdo other missions in beautifying their churches and enriching their services.[23]

David Weber has observed that America's Indians "cooperated only when they believed they had something to gain from the new religion and the material benefits that accompanied it, or too much to lose from resisting it." [24] As the seventeenth century proceeded, increasing numbers of Florida's Indians calculated—perhaps correctly—that their chances of survival were better out of the missions than in them. Numerous converts, particularly Guales and Timucuas, "abandoned their towns to retire among the heathen," who offered them liberty of livelihood as well as religion. Many more escaped only through death, as Spanish-borne diseases were spread wildly and widely through concentrated Christian settlements by mobile Christian laborers and porters. By 1675 Apalachee had lost at least 15,000 people, largely to plague, measles, and smallpox. Fourteen years later, Timucua's population was only 2 percent of what it had been when the Spanish arrived. Several of these outbreaks preceded and obviously helped to precipitate major revolts in Apalachee in 1647 and in western Timucua nine years later. Spanish and loyal Indian reprisals against the rebels only added to the long bills of native mortality.[25]

The causes of these uprisings tell us a great deal about the costs of conversion; bioarchaeologists tell us more. The Apalachee rebellion was essentially a civil war: traditional chiefs attacked newly Christianized chiefs in hopes of halting Spanish encroachment on their lives and liberties. In official postmortems, the forced labor system, particularly the hauling of burdens to St. Augustine and back, was indicted most heavily. The natives long remembered that when two hundred Apalachees carried loads to the capital in Governor Ruytiner's day, only ten returned home because the rest had died of starvation on the way. Throughout the century, traditionalists refused to jump on the Christian bandwagon because, they said, "on their becoming Christian the Spaniards treat them as slaves, . . . they no longer have liberty, nor are they masters of their possessions." [26]

The Timucua revolt of 1656 was ignited by similar provocations. Worst of all was the impressment of several chiefs and headmen, who were legally exempt from such indignities. No Spanish dons would tolerate being "burdened as if they were mules or horses" nor did their Indian counterparts. For eight months the offended Timucuas simply abandoned their resident friars until the latter gave up and left. Guale militiamen who returned home to defend their villages against possible Timucua attack were summarily deprived of their annual gifts and their weapons. In a petition to the governor, their chiefs spoke forcefully for their fellow Christians in the other two provinces. Their first target was the labor draft. "We have more vassals in the service of the governor and the soldiers," they complained, "than we have in our towns. For this reason, and the pestilences, we are nearly out of people: the wives lack husbands, the sons lack fathers, and the fathers lack sons. . . . More than 60 unmarried women . . . cannot marry because all the bachelors . . . are detained. . . ." Moreover, the soldiers stationed in their towns "order and govern us like absolute lords . . . [and] often they lay hands on us and treat us like dogs." It is small wonder that during the later English-Creek raids, runaway mission Indians struck themselves on the forehead and exclaimed: "Go away water! I am no Christian!"[27]

Although no contemporaries noticed them, archaeologists have traced in mission populations a number of skeletal problems that reflect a serious decline in native health. The culprits were the increased sedentism and density of mission settlements, greater reliance on corn, and the labor draft. More populous, less mobile villages led to contaminated water supplies and lack of sanitation, which bred infections. The sucrose in corn led to a pronounced increase in dental caries, while a decline in variety of foods consumed, particularly fish, contributed to a rise in iron anemia. Carrying heavy loads led to greater incidence of osteoarthritis and joint degeneration, especially of the spinal vertebrae.[28] The Indians who could not stand to "live under the bell in law and righteousness" and lit out for pagan territory may have prolonged their lives as well as secured their liberty, even as they denied themselves the consolations of a Church burial and a long rest in the Christian heaven.[29]

Those who stayed behind must have begun to doubt their choice after 1680 when the English in Carolina unleashed their Indian allies on the Spanish missions along the Guale coast, looking for slaves and seeking to eliminate any challenge to their economic hegemony in the Southeast. In five years all of the Guale missions had retreated to within fifty miles of St. Augustine. Then Yamasees and Lower Creeks, well supplied with firearms by their English trading partners, began a prolonged series of raids on the rest of La Florida. In 1702 Governor James Moore led an amphibious attack on St. Augustine that failed to seize the capital within the castillo but captured five hundred Indians.[30]

Two years later, after losing the governorship, Moore returned overland with more than 1,000 Indians to make two more strikes that virtually erased the Christian Indian presence from Florida outside the pinched environs of St. Augustine. Hundreds of faithful Indians were killed, at least 1,000 were enslaved, and perhaps 1,300 accompanied the invaders back to Carolina to live as English clients and to serve as a buffer on the colony's southern flank, all without benefit of clergy. Those enslaved were sold to planters in Carolina and in English colonies as far north as New England; perhaps a few ended up in the West Indies. In all, fourteen major doctrinas were reduced to ashes and deserted; several friars were killed in the process. The survivors fled east to Timucua and soon St. Augustine, west to Pensacola and the new French colony at Mobile, and north to be adopted by their pagan enemies and to reunite with captured kin. In 1708, the Spanish governor confessed that English Indians were slave-raiding with impunity all the way to the Keys and in the past several years had carried off between 10,000 and 12,000 Indians.[31]

From Colonel Moore's point of view, Carolina had been made safe for aristocracy. Apalachee, the last bastion, was so reduced, he gloated, that " it neither can supply St. Augustine with Provisions, or disturb, damage or frighten Our Indians living between us and Apalatchee, and the French. In short we have made Carolina as safe, as the Conquest of Apalatchee can make it."[32] But of course Carolina was never in danger from its southern neighbors. Even the Franciscans had no designs on England's allies after a half-hearted attempt to missionize the Apalachicolas and Chacatos northwest of Apalachee, and the mission Indians, even if they had had military urges, owned relatively few guns and were kept on a short tether in their towns. As Christians, they were even prohibited from scalping their enemies, an allegedly "diabolical custom" born of the "primitive paganism" they had forsworn. That removing the enemy's scalp forever deprived him of his soul or life force was lost on the fastidious Spaniards who directed the feeble defense of the missions and their native inhabitants.[33]

The destruction and scattering of La Florida's Indian population, therefore, was unnecessary and far from inevitable. Yet, at the same time, it may have been predictable. The behavior and attitudes of the Carolina English shown in the late seventeenth century were clearly visible in the opening acts of England's colonization of the Southeast, and their effects on the native cultures they touched were, tragically, almost the same.

The English investment of the Southeast began on Roanoke Island in the 1580s when Ralegh sponsored three attempts to plant a colony on its unprepossessing shores. While none of the colonies is likely to have lasted more than a year, even the brief appearance of the English altered the region's native lives in ways that would become a virtual pattern in other parts of the English South.

After an initial honeymoon period of gift-giving, trade, and cautious assessment, in which the local natives tried to enlist the newcomers in their preexisting factional or intertribal feuds, the English quickly proved to be poor neighbors and unreliable allies. They never brought or produced enough food to remain independent, so they pressured the natives to share their sometimes precarious corn caches when they could least spare them. With some competence in the Algonquian language of the area, acquired from two Indians purloined on a reconnaissance voyage in 1584, Thomas Harriot sought to sell the locals on the benefits of Christianity at the expense of their traditional shamans. A few natives applied to the English god without abandoning their own deities when inexplicable ailments began to crucify most of the villagers the English visited. "The people began to die very fast," Harriot noticed, and survivors were persuaded that the angry English were shooting them with "invisible bullets."[34]

To make matters worse, the English committed several acts of injustice or stupidity that united the locals against them. On the first voyage to the Outer Banks, the colonists burned a native village and its fields when villagers did not return a silver cup allegedly stolen from the visitors. They kidnapped and held prisoner a neighboring chief and his son to extract information against the colony's immediate neighbors and hosts, who were driven off the island by the

Englishmen's crowding and demands. The colonists failed to distinguish friends from enemies and twice attacked potential or actual allies. And near the end of the first year, Harriot, at least, regretted that "some of our companie . . . shewed themselves to[o] fierce, in slaying some of the people, in some townes, upon causes that on our part, might easily ynough have bene borne withall." A full-scale uprising in 1586 was the result, as were sour relations thereafter until the last colony disappeared from the landscape and the record.[35]

English colonizers seem to have learned precious little about cultivating good relations with natives when they transferred their energies and hopes to Virginia in 1607. Within forty years, the native population had been swept from the Tidewater, less by disease than by land-hungry planters and military conquest after futile uprisings. Powhatan's potent Mississippian-style chiefdom, which had met the invaders head on, lay in shambles, never to rise again. The tribal remnants that survived were pushed onto small reservations at the margins of the colony, and future chiefs were selected or approved by the victors and paid tribute to the governor at Jamestown. Tobacco grew in their deserted fields and villages, increasingly tended by black slaves from Africa and the West Indies. By 1700, the native population of eastern Virginia had fallen 87 percent to only 1,900; by no coincidence, whites and blacks together numbered 60,000.[36]

The difference between English and Spanish colonization of the Southeast could not have been starker. English settlement, initially in the hands of a joint-stock company, was primarily economic; particularly after the importation of sweet West Indian tobacco around 1612, newcomers competed with natives for fertile bottomlands. English immigration was voluminous and steady—despite a mortality rate before 1624 of *80 percent*—and consisted increasingly of fecund families rather than single male servants.[37] Unlike the Spanish, with their legal regard for native rights, the English never acknowledged the Powhatans' rights to land or sovereignty. They landed with royal charters to American soil and proceeded to rename—and thereby claim—every geographical feature on their imperial maps.[38] In a farcical scene, they even tried to make the haughty Powhatan kneel in feudal vassalage to King James, of whom he knew nothing and cared less.

Perhaps the greatest contrast with the Florida Spanish was that, despite sweet promises in several charters, the Virginians made virtually no attempt to convert the natives to Christianity. Their signal success was Pocahontas, who was kidnapped as a hostage, placed in the home of an Anglican minister, and converted in time to marry the young widower Rolfe in a church ceremony. More typical was the advice of the Rev. Jonas Stockham, who was persuaded that "till their Priests and Ancients have their throats cut, there is no hope to bring them to conversion."[39]

Although distasteful to modern sensibilities, the Reverend Stockham's recommendation made some political if not religious sense, considering the predicament the colonists had gotten themselves into. They had landed—actually, trespassed—on Jamestown Island, whose malarial swamps and salt-laden waters lay in the middle of one of the most powerful Indian polities in eastern America. During the last quarter of the sixteenth century, when the Mississippian chiefdoms of the lower South had largely disintegrated, Powhatan had pushed and palavered six inherited tribes into a paramount chiefdom of thirty-some tribes, between 13,000 and 14,000 people, including 3,200 warriors—not at all inferior to Coosa and Cofitachequi of old.[40] Although he was interested in trading corn for a few English goods, especially prestige items such as shiny copper and blue glass beads and useful metal tools and weapons, he would not sell his birthright for any price.[41] Off and on for the colony's first six years, he waged diplomatic and real warfare against the intruders. When he died in 1618, five years after Pocahontas's marriage brought an uneasy peace, his brother Opechancanough succeeded him and kept a suspicious eye on the acquisitive English, who built him an English-style house with a lock to buy his acquiescence in their expansion. But he, too, could not be bought, certainly not for a mess of cottage. In 1622 and again in 1644, Opechancanough brilliantly coordinated a surprise attack on the English settlements and farms in the Tidewater but, in the long run, to no avail. The Powhatans were reduced to tributary status and led a largely unacculturated life on the fringes of colonial society for the rest of the century. Some intermarriage with blacks may have Africanized a few native households, but the English guarded their ethnic purity by disdaining alliances with the defeated natives.[42]

With the demise of the Powhatan chiefdom, Virginians looked south and west for trade with the Indians of the Piedmont. Several exploratory trips into North Carolina and beyond in the next twenty-five years discovered native groups eager to swap furs and deerskins for European goods, a taste for which many had already acquired through direct or indirect trade with the Spanish in Florida.[43] The major funnel to these southern economies was through the Occanee-chis, whose island home in the Roanoke River and on the main north-south Indian path through the Piedmont endowed them with special status and power as middlemen. When Nathaniel Bacon's troops decimated them in 1676 during his eponymous rebellion, the trade conduit was left wide open for enterprising Virginians.[44]

Predictably, the Piedmont tribes, who before 1650 had been relatively untouched by world economic forces or disease, now found themselves battered by both. As more and more packhorse caravans jingled through their villages en route to the mountain Cherokees and other southern customers, native death rates climbed, villages contracted, moved, and incorporated remnants to stay viable, and their inhabitants grew increasingly dependent on coarse trading cloth, "Axes, Hoes, Knives, Sizars . . . Guns, Powder and Shot."[45]

But there was a limit to the Virginia traders' reach, made not only by distance and dangerous Indians. After 1670 the biggest obstacle was the new colony of Carolinians at Charles Town. Carolina was a royal gift of the restored Charles II to eight Lords Proprietor, who tried to govern the colony from England. Their English and largely Barbadian colonists, however, often had other ideas, particularly about Indian policy which directly affected their lives and fortunes. One of the colonists' first notions was to set local native groups against each other so they would not and soon could not unite against them. Complementary was their desire to begin a vigorous trade in Indian slaves, by which they could not only turn a quick profit but eliminate their most dangerous rivals for the region by transporting them to Virginia, New England, or the West Indies. Both of these plans displeased the Proprietors, who, if they could not draw quitrents from a colony of hardworking farmers and planters, sought at least to maintain a monopoly on the Indian trade and to outlaw the enslavement of Indians within four hundred miles of Charles Town unless taken in just wars. Needless to say, the ambitious ex-Barbadians who settled along Goose Creek found ways to circumvent both the Proprietors and the local governor and assembly.[46]

Their first maneuver was to neutralize any potential threat from the small coastal tribes and to clear title to their land by allowing the Westoes, a pugnacious confederated tribe living on the Savannah River a hundred miles west of Charles Town, to continue their murderous and allegedly cannibalistic raids on the coastal peoples. "As for [the Indians] att home," one of the Goose Creek men assured the Proprietors, "we have them in a pound, for to the Southward they will not goe fearing the Yamases," and "the Westoes are behind them a mortall enemie of theires . . . [;] of them they are more afraid than the little children are of the Bull beggers in England." A major reason for the Westoes' success was that they were "well provided with arms, [and] amunition . . . from the northward," that is, Virginia. Of even greater interest to the Carolinians was that the Westoes purchased their weapons, "tradeing cloath and other trade" goods with "drest deare skins, furrs, and young Indian Slaves." When the Westoes had outlived their usefulness to the colony by 1680, the Carolinians encouraged the Savannahs, a Shawnee band, and the Lower Creek tribes to move slightly eastward, to exterminate the Westoes, and to become the colony's new best friends.[47]

No matter who the favorite tribe was, they were expected to keep the merchant houses of Charles Town filled with deerskins and Indian slaves, which became the backbone of the Carolina economy until the advent of rice in the early eighteenth century and remained the foundation of several family fortunes long after.[48] Whatever the drawbacks of the Tidewater, Carolina's uplands were blessed with a geography for profit, which one enthusiast described as "a neighboring vast Indian Country affording large Quantities of Deer Skins." Even in the settlements, planters hired native hunters to supply their households with venison from seemingly "infinite Herds." In the interior and the mountains, deerskins became the standard unit of exchange. By the turn of the century, Governor Archdale could brag without exaggeration that "Charles-Town Traded near 1000 Miles into the Continent," at least to the Mississippi. A newly arrived French observer in the Mobile delta noticed that "the English were in those nations every day" in search of marketable deerskins and buffalo robes.[49]

But the French soldier went on to say that "the greatest traffic between the English and the natives [*sauvages*] is the trade of slaves . . . each person being traded for one gun." Either the Lower Louisiana price was low or the Chickasaws farther north enjoyed favored-nation status. In 1708, both Chickasaw and Talapoosie hunters were said to have earned "a Gun, ammunition, horse, hatchet, and a suit of Cloathes" for just one slave—a whole year's worth of deerskins. In turn, an Indian slave, frequently a woman or child, sold to a Carolina planter or out of the colony brought a handsome return to the English trader, even though an adult African might bring twice as much.[50]

For the Proprietors, the slave trade was fraught with moral and military dangers. Not only was the trade in distant war captives questionable, but free and tributary Indians in the colony were often clamped into slavery and shipped out before the law could rescue them. More dangerous perhaps was the traders' not-so-covert practice of fomenting "perpetual warrs . . . amon[g]st the Indians for the onely reason of making slaves." Both had the potential of bringing war into the colony, and "wars," the Proprietors knew, "are inconvenient to planters." But the Goose Creek faction and their ilk tried to argue that their Creek and Savannah allies were "so powerful that it [was] dangerous to disoblige them" and that "buy[ing] their slaves of them" kept the slaves "from a cruel death." They could even protest with straight faces that enslaving Indians was "a more Effectuall way of Civilising and Instructing [them], Then all the Efforts used by the french Missionaries."[51]

It was disingenuousness of such magnitude that allowed the Carolinians to incite their native allies and trading partners against the Spanish missions of Florida and to lead hundreds, perhaps thousands, of Indian converts into bondage. Unfortunately, the English had virtually no missionaries of their own to protest the wasting wars within the colony and without or to protect its native victims.[52] As one of the few, frustrated ministers clearly recognized, "Our Indian Traders are very much averse to see Missionaries among the Indians." [53]

In light of disease's utter disregard for borders or persons, the ultimate fate of the various native populations of the Southeast might look very similar. The vast majority of Indians succumbed to uncontrollable, unpredictable epidemics. But to the survivors, the treatment they received from their particular foreign invaders and neighbors made a crucial difference in the quality of and control over their lives. Whether the Apalachee converts or the Choctaw war captives who followed the Goose Creek men home to serve as branded slaves on English plantations or to be transported to chilly New England felt that their lives had changed for the better, we may never know, but we can certainly guess. Most of Powhatan's people were not alive to even hear the question. As for the other Indians of the Southeast, in our final chapter we will explore how they maneuvered to ensure their survival and to maximize their freedom and how the arrival of the French in Louisiana at once complicated and improved their chances.

III

MAKING DO

T H E relative decline of Spanish Florida in the eighteenth century might have seriously reduced native options in the Southeast had the French not moved into the Mississippi delta and valley after 1699. South Carolina continued to throw its weight around in native affairs, particularly as its burgeoning white and black population spread westward into the Piedmont. But the presence of the French in Louisiana, three major Indian uprisings, and the founding of Georgia in 1733 managed to slow if not completely check Carolina's grab for power in the Southeast. Despite the loss of its missions, Florida remained dangerous as "rebellious" tribes fled South Carolina for sanctuary with and war supplies from the Spanish at St. Augustine and Pensacola.

Because colonial power was, for the most part, evenly distributed and continental diplomats managed to give America long stretches of peace during the course of the eighteenth century, European competition for the Southeast was largely economic and the region's natives were the center of attention, at once the vehicle and the prize. Even the most chauvinistic politicians realized that no southern colony could survive, much less prosper, without the military assistance or armed neutrality of its native neighbors. As late as 1755, Edmond Atkin, soon to be the British superintendent of Indian affairs for the Southern Department, reminded the crown that " the prosperity of our Colonies on the [American] Continent, will stand or fall with our Interest and favour among [the Indians]. While they are our Friends, they are the Cheapest and strongest Barrier for the Protection of our Settlements; when Enemies, they are capable by ravaging in their method of War, in spite of all we can do, to render those Possessions almost useless."[1]

Colonial dependence on the Indians throughout most of the century gave many natives, particularly the distant, larger tribes, substantial (though never unlimited) room for maneuver and a relatively long lease on life, liberty, and land. Although their lives and cultures seemed decidedly impoverished in the eyes of their European neighbors, observers had to acknowledge that "No people in the World understand and pursue their true National Interest, better than the Indians."[2] A French governor made the point less objectively. "All the Indians," he told his superior, "know better than any people in the world how to take advantage of the need one has of them."[3] The natives' ability to play off the competing colonies allowed them to pursue what Edmond Atkin called their "Simple and Plain" national policy, which aimed at "Securing their personal Safety, a Supply of their Wants, and fair Usage."[4]

All of the southern colonies had two main objects: the first was to find, procure, and export products that were in short supply in the mother country; the second was to ensure the colonists' safety as they pursued their economic goals. Indians were essential to the attainment of both ends. In the first several decades of each colony, and even after the profitable export of rice, indigo, tobacco, and naval stores, beaver pelts and particularly deerskins supplied by the Indians were used to offset hefty debit columns in colonial accounts with European suppliers, many of which debts were incurred for large amounts of manufactured trade goods destined for native villages. These trade goods, in turn, secured for the colonies the natives' temporary alliance if not permanent allegiance. In the Southeast there was simply no other way to do so. Unlike in Canada and New England, neither the English nor the French employed enough missionaries or wielded enough spiritual clout to attract Indian allies with nonmaterial means. Governor James Glen of South Carolina recognized the colonists' predicament as clearly as anyone. In 1761 he told readers of his *Description of South Carolina* that "The Concerns of this Country are . . . closely connected and interwoven with *Indian* Affairs, and not only a great Branch of our Trade, but even the Safety of this Province, do . . . much depend upon our continuing in Friendship with the Indians. . . ." "It will be impossible to retain those *Indians* . . . in His Majesty's Interest," he went on, "unless we continue to trade with them."[5] At that juncture, according to Glen's reckoning, one in every eight Carolinians was involved in the Indian trade; their Indian customers made up two-thirds of the colony's inhabitants and supplied some 70,000 deerskins a year. Even after the colonists' separation from England, the half-Scottish Creek leader Alexander McGillivray reminded the Spanish in Florida that "Indians will attach themselves to & Serve them best who Supply their Necessities."[6] South Carolina agent Thomas Nairne had pressed the same point seventy-five years earlier: "They Effect them most who sell best cheap," he counseled. Indians "turn to those who sell them the best pennyworths."[7]

But the natives knew full well—and colonial traders had to learn the hard way again and again—that cost was not everything; "conveniency," quality, and especially "fair Usage" were equally if not more important.[8] English traders usually offered their goods at the lowest prices and paid the most for native deerskins, but they often lost their advantage through an excess of unregulated traders and cutthroat competition involving shady trading practices and abuse of customers. The French, by contrast, seldom had enough or the right sorts of trade goods at competitive prices to satisfy their customers, but they made up for some of these material deficiencies with exemplary conduct. Many English competitors were forced to admit that "No people Carries on ye Indian Trade in So Regular a manner as the French."[9] A Louisiana governor located the key to French policy when he wrote that "good faith in trading [not mere cost] . . . is the essential point and the strongest bond by which we can attach [the natives] to our side."[10]

For all the leverage the southeastern Indians gained from their ability to play the various colonial competitors against one another, the natives could not deflect forever the two heaviest weapons in the European arsenal: the spiraling growth of white and black populations in both the English and French colonies, and the lethal ravages of imported diseases that simultaneously consumed the native population. Peter Wood's careful census of demographic change in the colonial Southeast found that between 1700 and 1790, the Indians lost about 55 percent of their population while white and black numbers grew exponentially. In the older areas of white settlement east of the mountains, in Virginia, North Carolina, and South Carolina, the natives were reduced 95 percent, to some 800 people, while their immigrant competitors proliferated to over 1.3 million. Newly settled Louisiana experienced similar changes. In less than a century, the native population plunged 85 percent to just 4,000 while the total of blacks and whites exceeded 42,000.[11]

The only bright spot—a relatively dim one at that—was the backcountry between the mountains and East Texas. There the native presence was reduced only 48 percent by 1790, to some 48,000, though their white and black neighbors had multiplied from 1,600 to 237,000 in the same period, a five-to-one margin of superiority.[12] Against such odds, the natives of the Southeast had to learn to make do as best they could—to adjust some, often several, aspects of their lives to accommodate and to take advantage of the changing realities of the new South they shared, for better or worse, with Europeans, Africans, and, later, chiaroscuro Americans.

The major source of the Indians' attenuated success in the eighteenth century was the whitetail deer, which seemed to thrive equally well in Alabama canebrakes, Carolina meadows, and Appalachian forests. Thanks to sporadic cattle plagues in Western Europe, England and, less so, France turned increasingly to their American colonies for leather. In our own day of plastics and polyesters, it may be difficult to appreciate the manifold uses of leather in the early modern period. Students of Pope, Hume, and Voltaire will easily acknowledge the ubiquity of leather bookbindings, and mention of leather gloves, belts, and workingmen's aprons will surprise no one. But less familiar, perhaps, are buckskin breeches and coats for gents and proles alike, leather coverings of trunks, coach seats, and containers, leather buckets, leather hats (including one called "the South Carolina hat"), and leather horse tackle.[13] The leather market was big business, and America's natives shared in the action.

In 1764, to take a typical year, the southern colonies together shipped more than 800,000 pounds—400 tons—of deerskin to Europe, most of it from the ports of Charles Town and Savannah. Each skin weighed between one and three pounds. Undressed or "raw" skins obtained in the woods directly from Indian hunters were bought by the skin rather than by weight, the usual measure of the trade. "Half-dressed" skins, the most common, were denuded of flesh and hair by native women and given a quick smoking to prevent decay, but they often turned ripe in steamy warehouses before shipment and had to be beaten in the streets to expel vermin. The best prices went to skins that were "full dressed." After snouts, hooves, tails, and ears were trimmed off, the pelts were carefully smoked over corncob smudges, pounded with stones, and rubbed with deer brains to soften and preserve them. Customarily, these fine leathers ended up as tooled bindings in a gentleman's library, gloves for the opera, or a fancy frock coat.[14]

To obtain the various pelts from native hunters, the competing colonies had to found, finance, and regulate elaborate business organizations that stretched from European manufacturers, suppliers, and shippers to lowly packhorsemen and bilingual traders who operated as far as the Mississippi and often beyond. The headquarters of each organization was usually located in a colonial entrepôt—Charles Town, Augusta, New Orleans—where large merchant partnerships (in the English case) or a monopoly company (for a time in Louisiana) assembled the goods, credit, and personnel to launch expensive packtrains or convoys of pirogues deep into Creek, Chickasaw, Choctaw, or Cherokee country in search of skins.

After the Privy Council struck down South Carolina's public monopoly of the Indian trade in 1719, a hungry assortment of Virginians, Carolinians, and eventually Georgians, mostly undercapitalized and inexperienced, flooded the backcountry.[15] The inevitable result was bankruptcy for most and the concentration of the trade in the hands of relatively few large partnerships or companies. These firms placed trusted employees in major native villages or in convenient forts, where they usually married the daughters of chiefs or other important families to gain sponsors and protective kin. From their key locations, the traders not only fine-tuned the flow of trade goods and finessed the purchase of skins, but they also served their respective governments as ears, eyes, and tongues in the delicate and sometimes deadly game of intercolonial and intertribal politics. If a colonial competitor flooded the market with cheap goods or paid inflated prices for skins, or rumors of war circulated around native campfires, the trader was the first to know and to dispatch a letter, sometimes eccentrically spelled, to the capital with the intelligence.[16]

Although South Carolina and later Georgia instituted sensible systems of licenses, bonds for good behavior, and resident agents and roving commissioners in Indian country, the Indian trade continued to attract characters whose avidity for gain often outran their scruples and common sense. Sometimes the culprits were employees of the larger, more established firms, whose long-term investment in the trade could not countenance behavior guaranteed to alienate native customers and capable of inciting business-destroying war. But more commonly they were small-time adventurers in search of a quick buck (literally), heedless of how they got it. From the perspective of Indians, colonial officials, and seasoned traders alike, both varieties spelled trouble and were variously regarded as "Arab-like" "Horse Pedlars," "abandoned, reprobate, white savages," the "dregs and off-scourings of our colonies," and, least charitably, "monsters in human form, the very scum and out cast of the earth."[17]

The list of allegations against English traders is long, and, if true (as most seem to be), the behavior they describe seriously compromised the usual advantages the English enjoyed in supply, quality, and price. Colonial officials understandably worried when English traders sold goods to the French or Spanish enemy or to unfriendly tribes, such as the Choctaws, who made war on English allies, such as the Chickasaws.[18] They frowned equally on traders who incited intertribal wars in order to secure Indian captives for enslavement and sale (a trade that tapered off in the 1720s but had a long life) or who merely spread rumors of war to increase the sale of guns, ammunition, and war paint.[19] Although some Indian women might not have objected, the merchant-bosses of the Tidewater protested overeager traders who purchased quantities of untrimmed, undressed hides, which lacked the low-cost application of product-enhancing native labor. When Indian superintendent John Stuart negotiated a treaty between the Creek headmen and major Creek merchant-traders in 1767, one provision was that traders could accept only "four undressed skins in the hair" to every 150 pounds of "Indian dressed deerskins" because, he noted, "Trading for skins in the hair leaves room for great imposition of the Indians." He did not have to say that raw skins spoiled and generally brought much reduced prices in Europe.[20] Nor did his readers have to ask what "impositions" were possible. English sharpers had a wide reputation for playing fast and loose with what a Cherokee factor called "fals Stilliards, short Yards, and little Measures."[21]

Another dangerous practice was the overextension of credit to native customers. The credit system was firmly in place in the southern trade, as it was everywhere in North America, but it was subject to abuse, on both sides. Freebooting traders intercepted native hunters in the woods and relieved them of their skins before the Indians could reach the established traders in town who had advanced them supplies for the hunting season. Traders impatient with Indian debtors were known to steal a hunter's wife and children and sell them into slavery to settle his account. Indian tribes that built up impossible debts might decide that a war upon the creditors was the quickest way to clear the books. In 1715 the Yamasees and Creeks, one Carolinian recognized, "at once blott[ed] out all their Debts" by killing 90 of South Carolina's 100 traders.[22] Forty years later, a Carolina agent reported the Cherokees' growing dissatisfaction over the "Debts they owe[d]" and the unhappy choice they had between "paying them and cloathing themselves." They "are now ready," he warned, "to take all Measures . . . to get rid of their Debts," though he believed they had not yet talked of "killing the Traders," an option clearly on his and their minds.[23] Late in the colonial period, large tribal debts, particularly Creek, were settled by alienation of tribal territory to white creditors.[24]

The normal risks of doing business in a cross-cultural context were one thing; contemptible and even dangerous behavior on the part of individual traders was quite another. The low opinion of traders held by many Indians and couth Englishmen alike derived less from the traders' conduct of the trade per se—as slippery as that often was—than from their personal morality in Indian country. In 1715, David Crawley, a Virginian with extensive experience in the South Carolina trade, charged the southern traders with a host of crimes, all of which contributed to the outbreak of the deadly and destructive Yamasee War of that year. He had seen them enter native plantations and villages at will, kill hogs and fowl, and "take what they please without leave" or compensation, such as corn, peas, and watermelons. If the owners grumbled at these brazen robberies, the traders "threaten[ed] to beat and verry often did beat them verry cruelly." Before horses were used regularly to convey goods and skins, traders commandeered native porters to carry 70, 80, or even 100-pound packs 300, 400, or 500 miles and "pay[d] very little for it." To add insult to injury, "when [the traders] had sent the [native] men away about their busnes or they were gon ahunting," Crawley had "heard them brag to each other of debauching [the Indians'] wives, sumtime force them," and once had seen it himself "in the day time don."[25]

Equally dangerous though more difficult to diagnose was the behavior of employees like Charles Jordon among the Creeks. In August 1752 "he got drunk and quarreled with the Indians, striped naked, painted himself all over, and r[a]n about [Utchee] Town like a Madman with his Gun in his Hand, telling the Indians that he would now be revenged upon them for all the ill Usage he had received, that he did not care if they did kill him, that his Death would soon be revenged for there was an Army of white People coming up to cutt them all off." Apparently, this was no temporary aberration because the Creek agent had been told that Jordon "has often before endangered both his own Life and every white Man's in the Nation by his mad Actions. . . . Nor is he the only one," the agent continued; "there are several Others that are fitter for Bedlam or New Gate [prison] than to be trusted in an Indian Country where the Lives of many may very much depend upon their Behaviour."²⁶ On the native scale of outrage, traders who made off with Indian horses, mixed too much water in the trade rum, passed off inferior red lead as true vermilion, or allowed their own live-stock to dine on Indian gardens scored much lower, though never low enough to be forgiven entirely by people famous for long memories and immense pride.²⁷

By means and in manner somewhat different, the French in Louisiana collected about 50,000 deerskins a year—less than a third of South Carolina's best take—from 1720 until their political depar-ture in 1763. They managed to do this in spite of government reluc-tance and often inability to underwrite the trade, a monopoly com-pany's bankruptcy, lack of adequate settler capital to purchase trade goods from importers too few and too expensive, and relatively low demand and therefore prices for deerskins in France. Only after the crown built several military-trading posts among key Indian tribes, advanced trade goods on reasonable terms to individual set-tlers and soldiers, and reclaimed responsibility for government and defense in 1731 did the French earn a fighting chance to beat the English at the trading game, even among their closest and most proximate native allies.²⁸

Although French traders were not angelic contrasts to their English counterparts—there were too many uninhibited Canadian voyageurs in the colony for that—they did have the sense to realize that alienating their few allies and customers, even if watchful commandants had allowed it, was poor business and poorer diplomacy. So they molded their tongues to tribal languages or the Mobilian trade jargon, the region's *lingua franca*, learned the patient protocol of the calumet ceremony (which often lasted three days), and adapted themselves to the natives' strong preference for fixed price schedules.[29]

For its part, the government sought to compensate for inadequate and pricey shipments of trade goods with other kinds of largesse. According to their English rivals, the Louisianians gained the affections of their Indian customers primarily with "the Provision of Gunsmiths" gratis and "not so much valuable Presents as a judicious Application of them" in Indian country, in native villages, in annual congresses at Mobile, or at convenient forts. "The French by a constant prudent Practice," noted an envious Edmond Atkin, "make even Trifles productive of the most desirable National Consequences."[30] Careful to avoid the appearance of paying tribute to the tribes, French officials annually conferred guns, ammunition, and fancy outfits on selected leaders, especially "medal chiefs," and warriors who had served the French well, being particular to favor "old Head Men of Note" and orators who would remember the generosity of the French in town house and council. (English gift-givers tended to bypass such ancients in favor of younger hunters who could supply them with deerskins, and to require most recipients to make long treks to disease-ridden Charles Town and Augusta to receive them.)[31] So punctilious were the French in making presents that, on more than one occasion, they were forced to purchase several from their better supplied English competitors.[32]

The final advantage the French enjoyed was their missionaries, who were, according to Edmond Atkin, "almost of as much Consequence as Garrisons. They have been," he argued, "the means of gaining as much respect from the Indians to the French, as our Traders have caused disrespect to us, by their disolute Lives and Manners." Governor Bienville noted their uses in 1726 when he told the French Minister of Marine that, "in addition to the knowledge of God that they would impart to them . . . nothing is more useful than a missionary to restrain the Indians, to learn all that is happening among them [and] to inform the commandants of the neighboring posts about it, to prevent the quarrels that may arise between the voyageurs and the Indians, and especially to see to it that the former do not sell their goods at too high prices."[33]

If it is now clear that the colonists needed the Indian trade for profit and protection, we have only to establish why the Indians participated so avidly in the colonial trade. Contemporaries thought they knew the answer. As early as 1679, Virginia's John Banister told an English correspondent that "since there has been a way layd open for Trade . . . many Things which they wanted not before because they never had them are by that means become necessary both for their use and ornament." At the end of the colonial period, naturalist William Bartram put a heavily moral twist on his explanation when he concluded that the southeastern tribes "wage eternal war against deer and bear, to procure food and cloathing, and other necessaries and conveniences; which is indeed carried to an unreasonable and perhaps criminal excess, since the white people have dazzled their senses with foreign superfluities."[34]

Both observers were correct to suggest that, before the advent of Europeans and their trade, the Indians were perfectly capable of supplying all of their material needs from the natural resources available in the Southeast. But the order of acculturation they outline— from necessities through conveniences to luxuries—should be exactly reversed. All over North America, natives were given as gifts and then made their first purchases of what traders called "baubles" or "trifles," small goods usually of decorative or aesthetic value, such as hawk's bells, glass beads, finger rings, colored caps, even playing cards and broken pottery shards.[35] None of these things altered the basic ways of native living; they were, in Bartram's word, "superfluities," though nonetheless desirable for their novelty.

The next and final round of purchases simply and sensibly procured a variety of labor-saving "conveniences," tools or clothing or housewares that duplicated perfectly functional native items but were made from technologically or aesthetically superior materials, such as woven cloth, glass, or iron. There was no class of trade goods that we can objectively call "necessities." Only human users transform "conveniences" into "necessities" by changing their psychological need for and dependence upon those goods. The only absolute material necessities of life are food and water; everything else is either a nice convenience or a superfluous luxury.

A scene from William Bonar's 1757 map of the Creek Nation
shows an Indian couple sporting several European trade items.
The woman wears a striped duffel blanket and a hair ribbon.
The warrior carries a musket, metal-tipped spear, and iron
tomahawk and wears garters and a plume in his scalplock.
*Reproduced with permission of the Controller of Her Majesty's
Stationery Office, courtesy of the British Public Record Office,
C0700/Carolina 21.*

A Indien Camp.

Philip von Reck's pencil drawing of a southeastern Indian
hunting camp in 1736 shows two trade kettles and at least one
gun, used to gather the deerskins stretched and drying on the
lean-to poles.   *Courtesy of the Royal Library of Denmark,
Copenhagen, Manuscript Department, catalog signature Ny kgl.
Saml. 565, 4°.*

Von Reck's 1736 watercolor drawing of "Indiens going a hunting" shows change and persistence in native garb and equipment. The hunter on the left wears a painted leather matchcoat and carries a bow and arrow. The middle figure wears a white woolen trade blanket with red stripes and blue stroud leggings; he carries a metal kettle in his pack, a musket, and "A bottle in which they generally carry rum or brandy." The pipesmoking third man wears traditional leather leggings and moccasins, but his short leather jacket seems to have been tailored to European fashion. *Courtesy of the Royal Library of Denmark, Copenhagen, Manuscript Department, cat. sig. Ny kgl. Saml. 565, 4°.*

This 1736 watercolor drawing of a Yuchi busk ceremony by
Von Reck features native dancers wearing red and blue duffel
breechclouts, the gift of Georgia's founder James Oglethorpe.
Five trade muskets hang from the cypress-covered lodge.
*Courtesy of the Royal Library of Denmark, Copenhagen, Manuscript
Department, cat. sig. Ny kgl. Saml. 565, 4°.*

Von Reck's watercolor drawing of the Yuchi chief Senkaitchi and his wife illustrates the inroads made by European trade cloth in 1736, three years after the Georgia colony was founded. The woman wears a white blanket with red stripes, while her husband sports a red duffel breechclout and dark blue leggings beneath a traditional buffalo robe. Facial and body tattoos like the chief's would soon be made with imported gunpowder. *Courtesy of the Royal Library of Denmark, Copenhagen, Manuscript Department, cat. sig. Ny kgl. Saml. 565, 4°.*

The supreme war chief or captain of the Yuchis, Kipahalgwa, as painted by Von Reck in 1736. An open white shirt, not tucked in for lack of trousers, and red duffel leggings (and probably breechclout) suggest the native adaptation of European trade goods to traditional uses and preferences. The red paint used to color his eyes, noses, and short scalplock was probably already imported vermilion rather than native vegetable dye. *Courtesy of the Royal Library of Denmark, Copenhagen, Manuscript Department, cat. sig. Ny kgl. Saml. 565, 4°.*

Among the Indians, cloth and metal tools were quickly recognized as the greatest conveniences and most in demand. In one of the last years of the French regime in Louisiana, the annual list of presents for native allies included 15,800 ells (about 18 × 45 inches each) of limbourg cloth (half red, half blue), 1,020 blankets (worn as substitutes for buffalo or deerskin robes known as "match-coats"), 806 men's shirts ("as long in the front as in the back" because they were never tucked in), and 200 ells of finer scarlet cloths to make fancy outfits for "medal chiefs" (who, like most Indians, preferred loose breechclouts or "flaps" and detachable leggings to restrictive European-style trousers). And these were only the goods being *given* away. For trade with the Choctaws and six other tribes, the French had ordered 17,000 ells of limbourg, 19,400 blankets, 10,300 men's shirts, and 1,700 women's shirts.[36] Native customers of the English bought even more. So desirable was cloth that some natives were content to purchase second-hand clothing from other Indians who had easier access to the trade. When the Choctaws could not get enough cloth from the French during the naval blockades of the last intercolonial war, fifty of them circumvented French orders not to trade with the English by swapping skins for the "old Cloaths" of the Alabamas, who then obtained new ones from the English traders operating in Creek country.[37] Even shreds and tatters of trade cloth were desirable. Native women bought the lint and litter from traders' packs to make scarlet dye with which to color the duller and less expensive linens and cottons offered by the traders.[38]

The result of these wardrobe changes can be seen in contemporary pictures of natives *en scène*. Thomas Nairne's verbal portrait of Chickasaw women in 1708 requires little imagination. They "look sparkling in the dances," he wrote, "with the Cloaths bought from the English" and were "very loath any different should happen, least they again be reduced to their old wear of painted Buffeloe Calf skins."[39] Several watercolor sketches by Moravian visitor Philip Von Reck all show Georgia Creek costumes in 1736 that reflect the persistence of native styles with the addition of imported materials. Both men and women are wrapped in white trade blankets edged with red stripes, but blankets had not completely replaced intricately painted buffalo robes. Yet virtually everyone wears red or blue stroud cloth leggings, knee-length skirts, or breechclouts. The women also sport flowing red ribbons in their hair, as does a blanketed

Creek woman in William Bonar's 1757 drawing that accompanies his wonderful map of the Creek Nation. Leather moccasins were obviously preferred in the forests and swamps of the Southeast, and remained so until a turn in the native economy found a use for heavier soled shoes.[40]

Indian men and women altered their wardrobes not because they wanted to ape their European "betters"—clearly they did not want to and did not consider them superior—but simply because woven cloth had qualities superior to their traditional skin clothing. With scissors, needles, thimbles, and thread obtained in the trade, native women could more easily cut and sew their clothing. Moreover, they no longer had to laboriously tan several cumbersome and smelly skins before beginning the process; fewer raw or half-dressed deer-skins could purchase cloth that was not only brighter and more col-orful, but always soft, warm, and pliable even after getting wet. If they cared to wash the clothes before they wore out, they could; with skin garments they could not.

Von Reck's and Bonar's drawings also document the impor-tance in native lives of metal trade goods, both weapons and house-hold items. Bonar's Creek warrior wears only a cloth flap, war paint, arm and wrist bracelets, ribbon garters, and a plume in his topknot—all provided by French or English traders. But in addi-tion to a bow, a quiver of arrows, and a metal-tipped spear, he totes an iron tomahawk in his belt and a long musket—upside down and barrel first—over his shoulder. Two of Von Reck's Creek men also carry bows and arrows, but one blanketed hunter has a musket in one hand, a rum bottle in the other, and a trade kettle in his back-pack. Two other views of an open hunting lodge show three kettles on or near the fire and a row of five guns hanging muzzles down along one side.[41]

Trade inventories and archaeology suggest that these pictures do not lie. In 1759 the French planned to distribute as presents 2,440 woodcutters' knives, 1,200 clasp knives, 400 pairs of scissors, and 150 brass kettles, "large and medium, no small, larger at the top than at the bottom" to satisfy native preferences. They also sent into Indian country 8,000 pounds of "flat iron for hatchets, pick-axes, and tomahawks," to be hammered into shape by military post blacksmiths or perhaps by the Indians themselves. In trade the south-eastern Indians also wanted copious quantities of awls, fire steels (strike-a-lights), hoes, tin pots, sewing supplies, razors, and brass and iron wire.[42] All of these items were mere "conveniences"; they allowed the natives to do the things they had always done with less effort and with gains in efficiency and durability. While the materials were new, the shapes, functions, and meanings of the objects were virtually unaltered.

But the Indians no less than the colonists had a right to acquire new tastes, to form new aesthetic preferences, without our fretting over the decline of some imagined aboriginality. And they exercised it. We should expect no less of cultures that were experiencing a consumer revolution every bit as profound as the one their British colonial neighbors were undergoing simultaneously, particularly since the Indians' revolution had begun at least fifty years earlier than the Brits'.[43] Sooner or later, some daring Creek or Cherokee individualist had the courage or temerity to adopt a new fashion first seen in cosmopolitan Charles Town or New Orleans or in the home or on the person of the native wife of a local trader. If he or she was a respected leader, a chief or warrior or clan mother, the change in fashion would probably spread more rapidly, just as it would in London or Paris if the queen or a noble took the first step. How else can we explain the Creeks' adoption late in the eighteenth century of items of Scottish dress or the wrap-around turban of brightly colored cloth that men affected for many years? They were certainly under no more compulsion to flatter their American neighbors than they were earlier in the century, and no settlers that we know of wore turbans.[44] And how else can we understand the vast array of plain and fancy European cups, jugs, plates, bowls, and serving dishes — creamware, slipware, faience — that the Tunicas, the staunchest French allies, took to the grave in their Mississippi village between 1731 and 1764? Unlike most southeastern tribes, they preferred them to native pottery, they could afford to buy them, and they did so.[45]

The metal tool that enabled the Indians to bring down white-tail deer in sufficient numbers to purchase the other trade goods was, of course, the gun, at 12 to 16 dressed skins the costliest item on the native shopping list. The typical trade gun was lighter, cheaper, and shorter than most European guns. The Indians preferred them to "heavy buccaneer's muskets," said a French official, "because people who are always running through the woods wish nothing except what is very light."[46] In 1759 the French expected to hand out 500 30-caliber trade guns to allies and to trade nearly 4,000 more, in addition to 14 tons of powder, 40,000 flints, and 14,400 gunworms (for extracting wads). The lead for shot came not from Europe but from the famous Galena mines in the Illinois country, which was under Louisiana's aegis.[47]

Since most of the French trade was conducted on or near rivers, the Louisianians were easily able to supply their native customers with munitions. Even the English conceded French superiority in the ammunition trade "by means of their Water Carriage; whereas [English] Traders, being obliged to carry their Goods many hundred Miles upon Horses, [and] consulting their greatest Proffit, only carry but scanty supplies of that heavy Article and of small Value."[48] In 1741 a young French soldier tried to convince his Cherokee captors that, though French guns cost twice as much as English ones, they were better and more durable, and that "a pound of [French] powder had twice as much effect as a pound of the English." Cherokee warriors who received any of the anticipated French supplies on the eve of their 1760 uprising against the English may indeed have felt the extra kick in the special shipment of "powder for war," more potent than that needed to bring down a deer.[49] If, four years earlier, they had also been able to talk Virginia into furnishing them with accurate, long-range rifles like those the French allegedly supplied *their* allies, they would have had firepower at least equal to that of their Carolina enemies. English officials were reluctant to sell the Indians anything but smoothbore muskets because they foresaw that rifles put the Indians "too much upon an Equality with us in Case of a Breach." Most traders probably cared more that they punched larger holes in their whitetailed merchandise.[50]

While guns were, in one sense, only more powerful bows, two other novel and popular trade goods left deep marks upon native society in the eighteenth century, one subtly, one not so. Few observers noticed the quiet revolution wrought by the humble hand mirror, framed in wood or leather and worn around the neck or wrist of every warrior.[51] We who are so used to grooming ourselves in mirrors several times a day will find it difficult perhaps to imagine how people in the past must have felt in discovering their physical identities only through the eyes of others. The advent of portable mirrors enabled Indians for the first time to comb their own hair, apply their own war paint, and decorate their own scalp-locks, thereby undamming freshets of vanity and wellsprings of self-regard. Yet the new face in the mirror was not always comforting. During a smallpox epidemic in 1738, a "great many" Cherokees "killed themselves; for being naturally proud," wrote trader James Adair, "they are always peeping into their looking glasses . . . by which means, seeing themselves disfigured, without hope of regaining their former beauty, some shot themselves, others cut their throats, some stabbed themselves . . . many threw themselves with sullen madness into the fire. . . ."[52]

Possessed of equal power to destroy was alcohol—French brandy and English rum. Having, as with the mirror, no counterpart to alcohol in their culture, the Indians had to fashion their own rules for its use, but too often fell prey to its power. Most Indians drank to total inebriation; if every member of the group could not reach that goal, some abstained to ensure an adequate supply for the rest. Because they tended, under its influence, to commit all kinds of antisocial acts, even against their own kinsmen, they decided to blame the liquid or the seller, not the drinker. Despite periodic attempts by native leaders to prohibit its sale in their villages, customers and traders conspired to make it available. Since drunken Indians would "freely sell or part with any thing they have in the World (except their Wives and Children)" but not excepting their prized horses and their own long hair, traders were not reluctant to initiate their sales pitches with firewater. The traders might have earned kudos for "dashing" their liquor with water—one-third was the English "custom"—had they not charged full price for it and taken full advantage of its victims.[53]

Unfortunately, Indian traders as well as European cashed in on the profitably elastic native demand for spirits. Early in the century, the Tuscaroras traveled "several hundred Miles" westward to sell rundlets of watered rum by the mouthful for buckskins. Buyers appeared with bowls and the biggest mouthed friends they could find, but the sellers were only too ready to lambaste anyone who swallowed a drop, by mistake or design. William Bartram found equal humor in a Creek drinking fest in Florida. As bottles were passed freely around the circle, at least one native woman, "with an empty bottle, concealed in her mantle," takes "a good long draught, blushes, drops her pretty face on her bosom, and artfully discharged the rum into her bottle, and by repeating this artifice soon fills it: this she privately conveys to her secret store, and then returns to the jovial game, and so on during the festival; and when the comic farce is over," the woman "retails this precious cordial to them at her own price." [54]

While liquor and sharp trading did their part to separate native hunters from their hard-earned hides, two native customs also created a steady demand for imported merchandise. One was the Busk, the southeastern Green Corn Ceremony, during which the whole tribe assembled to begin a new year. On the first day, they collected "all their worn-out cloaths," housewares, and furniture and burned them in a huge bonfire. On the fourth and final day, they were allowed to don new clothes and reestablish their households with new paraphernalia, all of which the local trader was only too happy to furnish.[55] Similarly, the native habit of burying the dead with all their personal possessions boosted trader sales, particularly as personal accumulation grew in later decades. Kinsmen had to buy their own things in lieu of inheriting them. Only the Cherokees in the 1770s "entirely left off the custom" and bequeathed the deceased's effects to the "nearest of blood." According to James Adair, who had himself traded among them, they did so because of "the reiterated persuasion of the traders." We can only speculate on the cause of the peddlers' sudden and isolated fit of disinterestedness.[56]

For all its magnitude, both economic and geographical, the major effects of the European trade upon native society and culture did not flow from the sheer accumulation of foreign manufactures. The great majority of these items, we have seen, were only pleasing or superior substitutes for functional native-made goods, and their traditional meanings and uses were largely retained. The trade's major impact on the Indians resulted not from the *end* of the trade—the goods themselves—but from the *means* used to acquire them. The catalyst of change was not simply native acquisitiveness, but the Indians' pursuit of the game needed to purchase the new conveniences and luxuries, and their varied interactions with the colonial traders who brought the goods to their world.

If there is any doubt that traditional native values and uses were transferred to the new objects, we have only to look at the myriad

European goods that found their way into Indian graves. Many items accompanied their owners just as they had been purchased from the trader's pack, yet even they had obviously been used in ways more consonant with native culture than with European. Copper kettles were placed over the deceased's head as clay pots once were. Gunpowder made excellent (if volatile) tattoos. Coils of brass wire, sold on pencil-like spindles, served not only as trap wire and colonial duct tape, but as squeezable hair pluckers to rid native faces of unsightly and unintelligent beards.[57]

But more than a few grave offerings had been modified to fit traditional styles or functions or cannibalized for materials to fashion familiar objects. Former kettles, even new ones, became copper jewelry, arrowheads, and tinkling cones (for attachment to fringed clothing). Broken gun barrels, heated red hot, exacerbated the torture of war captives or were flattened to make hide scrapers and chisels. A brass milk skimmer was reborn as a gorget and duplicated in brass, down to the hole pattern, by the Indians; going the other way, the owner of a British gorget preferred a less martial crucifix. Like obsidian, glass bottle shards were chipped into scrapers and arrowheads. Used gunflints, some native-made, easily became strike-a-lights. A yellow slip-glazed candleholder was drilled to make a pipe bowl, while the lead seals from bales of English stroud were cut into pendants or melted and poured into carved-stone bullet molds.[58] No matter what form they took or what material they were made from, all of these objects were placed in graves, as personal possessions long had, so that their spirits would accompany the human spirits to the Land of the Dead, which resembled nothing so much as a familiar Indian village in the best of times.[59] Those beliefs and practices did not change in the colonial period, nor for many decades thereafter if at all.

The key to change in the native Southeast, then, lies not in the material end of the trade but in the social and cultural paths the Indians took to it. One of those paths led largely uncontrollable numbers of European and African strangers into the native world. In 1756 a Cherokee delegation to the Creeks indicated what that intrusion meant to them at that historical moment. "The English ha[ve] now a Mind to make Slaves of [us] all," they warned, "for [they] have already filled [our] Nation with English Forts and great Guns, Negroes and Cattle."[60] Their list is telling. While they accommodated traders and their desired wares, colonial forts on native land compromised native sovereignty and independence, threatened the natives' safety, and sheltered unscrupulous traders from the consequences of their actions. African servants might have provided the Indians with valuable object lessons in the loss of freedom, but English officials—not the French—did their best to separate the races lest they form "dangerous connections." For their part, most Indians did not welcome slaves into their villages because the blacks were used mostly to raise food for the traders, which deprived native women of that lucrative business.[61]

When they belonged only to traders, cattle were as unwelcome as slaves because they were unfettered, ate up native gardens, and drove out deer from their fixed territories. But beginning in the 1740s, cows also served the Cherokees as substitutes for diminishing deer and as sources of milk and butter, which they probably sold at the nearest English garrison. The vocabulary gathered by surveyor William De Brahm in the very year of the Cherokee delegation's complaint contains words for *cow, bull, calf, milk,* and *butter,* all derived from *wággaw,* the native rendition of the Spanish *vaca.* Before the end of the century, most southeastern tribes raised cattle or rustled them to compensate for diminished deer herds on diminished tribal lands.[62]

Other European livestock had a similar reception. Along with cattle and chickens, pigs had to overcome the natives' initial belief that natural properties were transfused into humans through the food they ate; "he who feeds on venison," James Adair explained, "is . . . swifter and more sagacious than the man who lives on the flesh of . . . helpless dunghill fowls, the slow-footed tame cattle, or the heavy wallowing swine." "When swine were first brought among [the Creeks]," Adair continued, "they deemed it such a horrid abomination . . . to eat that filthy and impure food, that they excluded the criminal from all religious communion in their circular town-house. . . . Now [in the 1770s] they seldom refuse to eat hogs flesh, when the traders invite them to it." Well before then, in fact, they and other tribes, particularly the Cherokees, were raising them for sale to the colonists and for their own consumption.[63]

Although horses were eaten in desperation (the Creeks and Choctaws called them "big deer"), most native families acquired them to carry their belongings to their hunting grounds and deerskins to the trading post. By the 1770s, Adair said, and probably thirty years before that, "almost every one hath horses, from two to a dozen; which makes a considerable number, through their various nations." Bred from handsome Andalusian stock in Florida and the Southwest, Indian horses allowed hunters to extend their range in search of more and more deer for market. When that extension brought families and tribes into collision with rivals, mounted warfare was often the result. And when the deer population petered out at the end of the century, male and even female horse thieves made a substitute living raiding native and American herds.[64]

The foreseeable depletion of the southeastern deer herds resulted not only from the natives' material desires but from a major change in their hunting ethic. Before deer hunting became big business, Indians killed only as many animals as they needed, they supplicated the master spirit of the species before killing and thanked it after, and they used all parts of the deer for food, clothing, ornaments, and weapons. In their gun-aided haste to harvest ever more skins for the trade, they soon omitted their religious obligations, and, lamented surveyor De Brahm, "they make a great Carnage among the Deers, kill them for the sake of their Skins, and leave their Carcasses [to rot] in the Forrests."[65]

The European competition for native allies and the surrogate war in trade that it fostered wrought many changes in southeastern Indian culture. Epidemic and epizootic diseases made heavy inroads on native populations.[66] Wars became deadlier because of guns and colonial scalp bounties; they became more frequent because of the trade in Indian slaves and America's involvement in European conflicts. Accordingly, civil chiefs lost authority and prestige to their warrior counterparts.[67] Native marriages to white and black traders and soldiers bred a new population of mixed-blood children, who often pushed traditionalists into innovations such as foreign fashions, formal education, personal accumulation, religious conversion, and chattel slavery.[68] Gender relations shifted with new roles in new economies.[69] Traditional crafts and skills were lost with the wholesale advent of goods manufactured abroad.[70] But the most serious change of all was the natives' increasing dependence on their colonial neighbors for economic viability and, by extension, their loss of political autonomy.

As early as 1681, the Lords Proprietor of South Carolina had an economic plan to dominate the Indians of their colony and beyond. "Furnishing a bold and warlike people with Armes and Ammunition and other things usefull to them," they informed their governor and council, "[would tie] them to soe strict a dependance upon us . . . that whenever that nation that we sett up shall misbehave . . . toward us, we shall be able whenever we please by abstaineing from supplying them with Ammunition . . . to ruine them." [71] That, of course, is exactly what happened, even though the English could not foresee that the arrival of the French would allow the natives of the Southeast to prolong their parole for several decades.

But sooner or later, the Indians themselves recognized that their new involvement in a global economy made them prisoners as well as players. At a conference in Charles Town in 1753, Skiagunsta of the Lower Cherokees told Governor Glen that "[I] have always told my People to be well with the English for they cannot expect any Supply from any where else, nor can they live independent of the English. What are we red People?" he asked. "The Cloaths we wear, we cannot make ourselves, they are made [for] us. We use their Amunition with which we kill Dear. We cannot make our Guns, they are made [for] us. Every necessary Thing in Life we must have from the White People." [72] The implications of that dependence were clearly seen by the "Tattoed Serpent," a Natchez war chief. "Why did the French come into our country?" he once asked a French neighbor. "Before they came, did we not live better than we do [now]? . . . In what respect, then, had we occasion for them: Was it for their guns? The bows and arrows which we used were sufficient to make us live well. Was it for their white, blue, and red blankets? We can do well enough with buffalo skins which are warmer. . . . In fine, before the arrival of the French, we lived like men who can be satisfied with what they have; whereas at this day we are like slaves, who are not suffered to do as they please." [73]

In 1764, British Indian superintendent John Stuart summed up the Indians' historical plight all too well. "The Original great tye between the Indians and Europeans was Mutual conveniency. [But] A modern Indian," he knew, "cannot subsist without Europeans. . . . So that what was only Conveniency at first is now become Necessity and the Original tye Strengthened." [74] A mutual bond had led to a kind of bondage for the natives, though in reality they were no more—or less—imprisoned by the capitalist world-system than were their European partners and rivals. But the native situation was indeed different, on two counts. First, the Indians' new world *felt* worse to them because their dependence—not just upon nature but now too upon anonymous strangers—was so new; the colonists could not remember a time when they were truly self-sufficient. And, second, when the "Mutual conveniency" that brought them together melted away after the American Revolution, the new Americans soon had no economic or political need for the Indian people (as distinguished from their land), while the Indians could never again live free of the American economy.

Before the colonists' declaration of independence, southern leaders were agreed that "it can never be our Interest to extirpate [the Indians], or to force them from their Lands" because "their Ground would be soon taken up by runaway *Negroes* from our Settlements, whose Numbers would daily increase, and quickly become more formidable Enemies than Indians can ever be. . . ."[75] Removing the 48,000 natives who inhabited and dominated the southern backcountry was simply not feasible in 1770 or in 1790. But within forty years, white America found it both necessary and convenient to do just that.

NOTES

INTRODUCTION: THE FIRST SOUTHERNERS

1. John Locke, *Two Treatises of Government*, ed. Peter Laslett (Cambridge: Cambridge University Press, 1960), 319. In this passage Locke refers specifically to the introduction of money, which enabled and encouraged the unequal aggrandizement of possessions, especially land. His general discussion treats man's emergence from the state of nature into civil society under law.

2. Western historians perhaps have been too ready to accept literally the testimony of European explorers that the first Indians they encountered in the Americas regarded them with amazement and awe as "gods." While the explorers might not have been wrong in their description of Indian behavior, we should not automatically assume that their choice of the word *gods* was apt or that the advent of white Europeans constituted a major irruption in native historiography. James Lockhart has shown that in the Mexican codices the arrival and military conquests of the Spanish barely appeared and did not alter the basic thrust and themes of native history-telling. James Lockhart, ed. and trans., *We People Here: Nahuatl Accounts of the Conquest of Mexico*, Repertorium Columbianum 1 (Berkeley and Los Angeles: University of California Press, 1993), 6, 12–21. For the more traditional view, see James Axtell, *Imagining the Other: First Encounters in North America*, Essays on the Columbian Encounter (Washington, D.C.: American Historical Association, 1991), 10–12; also Axtell, *Beyond 1492: Encounters in Colonial North America* (New York: Oxford University Press, 1992), 37–40.

I. THE SPANISH INCURSION

1. Samuel M. Wilson, *Hispaniola: Caribbean Chiefdoms in the Age of Columbus* (Tuscaloosa: University of Alabama Press, 1990).

2. Bruce D. Smith, "The Archaeology of the Southeastern United States: From Dalton to de Soto, 10,500–500 B.P.," *Advances in World*

Archaeology, 5 (1986), 53–63; Vincas P. Steponaitis, "Prehistoric Archaeology in the Southeastern United States, 1970–1985," *Annual Review of Anthropology,* 15 (1986), 387–93; Charles Hudson and Carmen Chaves Tesser, eds., *The Forgotten Centuries: Indians and Europeans in the American South, 1521–1704* (Athens: University of Georgia Press, 1994), 17–35, 125–253; Karl T. Steinen, "Ambushes, Raids, and Palisades: Mississippian Warfare in the Interior Southeast," *Southeastern Archaeology,* 11:2 (Winter 1992), 132–39; David H. Dye, "Warfare in the Sixteenth-Century Southeast: The de Soto Expedition in the Interior," in David Hurst Thomas, ed., *Columbian Consequences, Volume 2: Archaeological and Historical Perspectives on the Spanish Borderlands East* (Washington, D.C.: Smithsonian Institution Press, 1990), 211–22; Dye, "The Art of War in the Sixteenth-Century Central Mississippi Valley," in Patricia B. Kwachka, ed., *Perspectives on the Southeast: Linguistics, Archaeology, and Ethnohistory,* Southern Anthropological Society Proceedings, No. 27 (Athens: University of Georgia Press, 1994), 44–60.

3. James E. Kelley, Jr., "Juan Ponce de León's Discovery of Florida: Herrera's Narrative Revisited," *Revista de historia de America,* no. 111 (enero–junio 1991), 31–65 at 45, 49.

4. Paul E. Hoffman, *A New Andalucia and a Way to the Orient: The American Southeast During the Sixteenth Century* (Baton Rouge: Louisiana State University Press, 1990), chs. 1–2; Jerald T. Milanich, *Florida Indians and the Invasion from Europe* (Gainesville: University Press of Florida, 1995), 106–113.

5. David B. Quinn, ed., *New American World: A Documentary History of North America to 1612,* 5 vols. (New York: Arno Press and Hector Bye, 1979), 1:248 (Gómara); 1:266 (Martyr). See also Paul E. Hoffman on Ayllón in Hudson and Tesser, eds., *Forgotten Centuries,* 36–49.

6. *Cabeza de Vaca's Adventures in the Unknown Interior of America,* ed. and trans. Cyclone Covey (Albuquerque: University of New Mexico Press, 1983). Rolena Adorno and Patrick Pautz's definitive critical edition of Cabeza de Vaca's narrative will soon be published by University of Nebraska Press. See also Paul E. Hoffman in Hudson and Tesser, eds., *Forgotten Centuries,* 50–73, on the Narváez entrada.

7. Lawrence A. Clayton, Vernon James Knight, Jr., and Edward C. Moore, eds., *The De Soto Chronicles: The Expedition of Hernando De Soto to North America in 1539–1543,* 2 vols. (Tuscaloosa: University of Alabama Press, 1993), 1:48 (Gentleman from Elvas), 360 (royal contract). On Soto's entrada, see Hoffman, *New Andalucia,* ch. 4; Milanich, *Florida Indians and Invasion,* 127–36; Charles Hudson in Hudson and Tesser, eds., *Forgotten Centuries,* 74–103.

8. See Hoffman, *New Andalucia,* chs. 9–10; Milanich, *Florida Indians and Invasion,* ch. 8; Eugene Lyon, *The Enterprise of Florida: Pedro Menéndez*

de Avilés and the Spanish Conquest of 1565–1568 (Gainesville: University Presses of Florida, 1976, 1983).

9. Hoffman, *New Andalucia*, ch. 12; David Beers Quinn, *Set Fair for Roanoke: Voyages and Colonies, 1584–1606* (Chapel Hill: University of North Carolina Press, 1985).

10. Paul E. Hoffman, "A New Voyage of North American Discovery: Pedro de Salazar's Visit to the 'Island of Giants,'" *Florida Historical Quarterly*, 58:4 (April 1980), 415–26.

11. Quinn, ed., *New American World*, 1:259. See also Hoffman, *New Andalucia*, 3–18.

12. Hoffman, *New Andalucia*, 11, 20, 48 (Oviedo), 67. See *De Soto Chronicles*, 1:56, 58, for two Florida Indians who were captured by an advance party of Soto's *entrada* and escaped as soon as they were returned to their homeland.

13. Clifford M. Lewis and Albert J. Loomie, *The Spanish Jesuit Mission in Virginia, 1570–1572* (Chapel Hill: University of North Carolina Press, 1953), 15–18, 39–49; Charlotte M. Gradie, "Spanish Jesuits in Virginia: The Mission That Failed," *Virginia Magazine of History and Biography*, 96 (1988), 131–56; Gradie, "The Powhatans in the Context of the Spanish Empire," in Helen C. Rountree, ed., *Powhatan Foreign Relations, 1500–1722* (Charlottesville: University Press of Virginia, 1993), ch. 7.

14. *Cabeza de Vaca's Adventures*, ed. Covey, 32–33; Hugh Honour, *The New Golden Land: European Images of America from the Discoveries to the Present Time* (New York: Pantheon, 1975), 28–29. In the late seventeenth century, coastal Indians were still reaping profits from the material and human salvage of wrecked ships. See *Jonathan Dickinson's Journal; or, God's Protecting Providence* [1696–1697], ed. Evangeline Walker Andrews and Charles McLean Andrews (rev. ed. New Haven: Yale University Press, 1961).

15. Laura Branstetter, "Research of the [Montague] Tallant Collection: Final Report" (University of South Florida—New College, Senior thesis in Anthropology, May 1989), 9 (Tairona gold man and lizard, Sinu nose ring?), cat. no. A6736 (Colombian cast gold scorpion), A6952 (cast gold eagle pendant); Jonathan Max Leader, "Metal Artifacts from Fort Center: Aboriginal Metal Working in the Southeastern United States" (University of Florida, M.A. thesis in Anthropology, 1985), 74 (Incan jaguar and Quimbaya necklace ornaments).

16. Leader, "Metal Artifacts from Fort Center," 78–80; Branstetter, "Research of the Tallant Collection," 11–13, cat. no. A7041–7064 (silver beads from Spanish coins); Jeffrey M. Mitchem and Dale L. Hutchinson, *Interim Report on Archaeological Research at the Tatham Mound, Citrus County, Florida: Session III* (Misc. Project Report Series No. 30, Florida State Museum, Dept. of Anthropology, 1987), 55–59. For illustrations of

reworked silver artifacts, see Jerald T. Milanich and Susan Milbrath, eds., *First Encounters: Spanish Explorations in the Caribbean and the United States, 1492–1570* (Gainesville: University of Florida Press, 1989), 107, and Milanich, *Florida Indians and Invasion,* 42, 46, 47, 50, 51.

17. *Memoir of Dº. d'Escalente Fontaneda Respecting Florida. Written in Spain, About the Year 1575,* ed. and trans. Buckingham Smith (Washington, D.C., 1854; rev. ed. Miami: University of Miami and the Historical Association of South Florida, 1944), 18–20.

18. Gonzalo Solís de Merás, *Pedro Menéndez de Avilés . . . : Memorial,* ed. and trans. Jeannette Thurber Connor, Publications of the Florida State Historical Society, No. 3 (Deland, 1923; facsimile ed. Gainesville: University of Florida Press, 1964), 141, 144–45.

19. *Memoir of Fontaneda,* 19; Solís de Merás, *Pedro Menéndez,* 148; *Dickinson's Journal.*

20. *Memoir of Fontaneda,* 19–20.

21. Solís de Merás, *Pedro Menéndez,* 142, 151; Kathleen A. Deagan, "Mestizaje in Colonial St. Augustine," *Ethnohistory,* 20:1 (Winter 1973), 55–65: Eugene Lyon, "Cultural Brokers in Sixteenth-Century Spanish Florida," in *Spanish Borderlands Sourcebooks,* gen. ed. David Hurst Thomas, vol. 24: *Pedro Menéndez de Avilés,* ed. Eugene Lyon (New York: Garland, 1995), 329–36.

22. Charles Hudson, *The Juan Pardo Expeditions: Exploration of the Carolinas and Tennessee, 1566–1568* (Washington, D.C.: Smithsonian Institution Press, 1990).

23. Herbert I. Priestley, ed. and trans., *The Luna Papers: Documents Relating to the Expedition of Don Tristán de Luna y Arellano for the Conquest of La Florida in 1559–1561,* Publications of the Florida State Historical Society, No. 8, 2 vols. (Deland, 1928); Charles Hudson, Marvin T. Smith, Chester B. DePratter, and Emilia Kelley, "The Tristán de Luna Expedition, 1559–1561," *Southeastern Archaeology,* 8:1 (Summer 1989), 31–45; the letter is also in Milanich and Milbrath, eds., *First Encounters,* ch. 9.

24. Hudson *et al.,* "The Luna Expedition," 32.

25. *De Soto Chronicles,* 1:59, 62, 130 (Gentleman from Elvas), 225 (Biedma), 2:114, 116 (Garcilaso de la Vega).

26. Garcilaso de la Vega, educated and writing in Spain long after the events, said that Indian porters were "called *tamemes* in the language of the island of Española." Historian-editor Buckingham Smith, on the other hand, argued that the word derived from the language of "the Mexican Indians" (Nahuatl, presumably): *tlamama* or *tlameme,* someone who carried loads on the back. *De Soto Chronicles,* 1:194n.110, 2:278.

27. *Ibid.,* 1:154 (Gentleman from Elvas, my emphasis).

28. *Ibid.,* 1:229, 283, 291 (numbers of tamemes), 2:312, 400, 439 (feet crippling).

29. *Ibid.*, 1:74, 150, 153 (Gentleman from Elvas). By contrast, when Captain Pardo set out to "pacify" the territory northwest of Santa Elena twenty-five years later, he took only a hundred-some men and a large quantity of gifts to lubricate the voluntary payment of maize "tribute" to the Spanish and the building of separate lodgings by the Indian villagers he encountered. He even had the foresight to encourage a fertile village not far from Santa Elena to "sow a large quantity of [extra] maize" for future Spanish needs rather than commandeer every kernal they had, as the locust-like Soto entrada was wont to do. Hudson, *Juan Pardo Expeditions,* 293.

30. *De Soto Chronicles,* 1:89, 226, 238, 267, 268, 282–83, 285, 289, 303.

31. *Ibid.,* 1:120, 121 (Gentleman from Elvas), 303 (Rangel).

32. *Ibid.,* 1:289 (Rangel).

33. Axtell, *Imagining the Other;* also in Axtell, *Beyond 1492,* ch. 2.

34. *De Soto Chronicles,* 1:87, 141 (Gentleman from Elvas), 2:315 (Garcilaso de la Vega).

35. *Ibid.,* 1:94 (Gentleman from Elvas), 285 (Rangel); Woodbury Lowery, *The Spanish Settlements Within the Present Limits of the United States, 1513–1561* (New York: G. P. Putnam's Sons, 1911), 365.

36. Quinn, ed., *New American World,* 2:306, 353.

37. *De Soto Chronicles,* 1:70, 93 (chains), 95, 131, 272, 285, 286–87, 291 (gifts); Hudson, *Juan Pardo Expeditions,* 135–41, 266; Milanich and Milbrath, eds., *First Encounters,* ch. 7; Jeffrey P. Brain, "Artifacts of the Adelantado," *Conference on Historic Site Archaeology Papers,* 8 (1975), 129–38; Kathleen Deagan, *Artifacts of the Spanish Colonies of Florida and the Caribbean, 1500–1800* (Washington, D.C.: Smithsonian Institution Press, 1987).

38. *De Soto Chronicles,* 1:279–80 (Rangel). It is possible that Soto's men saw Spanish-style clothing that had been made from local deerskins by the beleaguered colonists themselves; most of their own supplies had been lost in a storm just as they landed.

39. *Ibid.,* 1:265 (Rangel). For its wider use in Spain and Latin America, see Luis Weckmann, *The Medieval Heritage of Mexico,* trans. Frances M. López-Morillas (New York: Fordham University Press, 1992), 111–13, 115n.20.

40. *De Soto Chronicles,* 1:158, 291, 293; R. B. Cunninghame Graham, *The Horses of the Conquest,* ed. Robert Moorman Denhardt (Norman: University of Oklahoma Press, 1949); Barbara A. Purdy, "Weapons, Strategies, and Tactics of the Europeans and the Indians in Sixteenth- and Seventeenth-Century Florida," *Florida Historical Quarterly,* 55:3 (January 1977), 259–76 at 267–68.

41. *De Soto Chronicles,* 1:66, 80, 146, 257, 262, 2:150–52, 459–60; Lowery, *Spanish Settlements,* 133–34 (Oviedo); Purdy, "Weapons, Strategies, and Tactics," 268–69; John Grier Varner and Jeannette Johnson Varner, *Dogs of the Conquest* (Norman: University of Oklahoma Press, 1983), esp. 104–110.

42. Robert L. Blakely, ed., *The King Site: Continuity and Contact in Sixteenth-Century Georgia* (Athens: University of Georgia Press, 1988), chs. 7-9; Blakely and David S. Mathews, "Bioarchaeological Evidence for a Spanish–Native American Conflict in the Sixteenth-Century Southeast," *American Antiquity*, 55:4 (1990), 718-44. At least two Indians interred in the Tatham mound in west-central Florida had been cut by Spanish swords. Mitchem and Hutchinson, *Interim Report on the Tatham Mound*, 9, 41.

43. *De Soto Chronicles*, 1:99, 122, 143, 152, 153, 235, 267, 292. When the Indians retaliated with arrows, Spanish armor—traditional metal and lighter weight quilted cotton and canvas—deflected them. The quilted armor, *escaupiles*, was copied from the Aztecs and became the standard defensive gear in sixteenth-century Florida among all Europeans. At the battle of Mabila, Soto's secretary, Rodrigo Rangel, took more than twenty arrows in his "quilted tunic of thick cotton" and suffered no harm. *De Soto Chronicles*, 1:293. See also Purdy, "Weapons, Strategies, and Tactics," 266-67.

44. *De Soto Chronicles*, 1:104, 135 (Gentleman from Elvas).

45. *Ibid.*, 1:145, 146-47, 244, 267.

46. *Ibid.*, 1:106, 150, 155, 229, 241, 256, 264, 301; Charles Hudson, "A Spanish-Coosa Alliance in Sixteenth-Century North Georgia," *Georgia Historical Quarterly*, 72:4 (Winter 1988), 599-626.

47. Dye, "The Art of War in the Mississippi Valley," 60n.16.

48. *Ibid.*, 50-53.

49. *De Soto Chronicles*, 1:106, 153 (Gentleman from Elvas), 2:262-63, 472, 498 (Garcilaso de la Vega). According to Garcilaso, Soto gave a male and a female pig to friendly caciques for breeding. *De Soto Chronicles*, 2:263.

50. Hoffman, *New Andalucia*, 53.

51. Alfred W. Crosby, Jr., *The Columbian Exchange: Biological and Cultural Consequences of 1492* (Westport, Conn.: Greenwood Press, 1972), ch. 3; Crosby, *Germs, Seeds, & Animals: Studies in Ecological History* (Armonk, N.Y.: M. E. Sharpe, 1994), chs. 2-3; Donna L. Ruhl, "Spanish Mission Paleoethnobotany and Cultural Change: A Survey of the Archaeobotanical Data and Some Speculations on Aboriginal and Spanish Agrarian Interactions in La Florida," in Thomas, ed., *Columbian Consequences*, 2: ch. 35; Ruhl, "Old Customs and Traditions in New Terrain: Sixteenth- and Seventeenth-Century Archaeobotanical Data from *La Florida*," in C. Margaret Scarry, ed., *Foraging and Farming in the Eastern Woodlands* (Gainesville: University Press of Florida, 1993), ch. 15; Francis Xavier Luca, "Culture and Ecology: Indians, Europeans, and Animal Husbandry in Colonial Florida," *Southern Historian*, 13 (Spring 1992), 7-23.

52. Menéndez also imported some 3,000 chickens and 2,700 fanegas of corn from Yucatán. Lyon, *Enterprise of Florida*, 183n.41.

53. The New World had only two chronic infectious diseases of any consequence—tuberculosis and treponematosis, both of which were prevalent in the precontact Southeast. Charles F. Merbs, "A New World of Infectious Disease," *Yearbook of Physical Anthropology*, 35 (1992), 3–42; John W. Verano and Douglas H. Ubelaker, eds., *Disease and Demography in the Americas* (Washington, D.C.: Smithsonian Institution Press, 1992), ch. 5.

54. Crosby, *Columbian Exchange*, ch. 2; Crosby, *Germs, Seeds, & Animals*, chs. 2–3, 5–7; Verano and Ubelaker, eds., *Disease and Demography in the Americas*, chs. 4–5, 17; George R. Milner, "Epidemic Disease in the Postcontact Southeast: A Reappraisal," *Midcontinental Journal of Archaeology*, 5:1 (April 1980), 39–56; Robert L. Blakely and Bettina Detweiler-Blakely, "The Impact of European Diseases in the Sixteenth-Century Southeast: A Case Study," *ibid.*, 14:1 (April 1989), 62–89. Henry F. Dobyns, *Their Number Become Thinned: Native American Population Dynamics in Eastern North America* (Knoxville: University of Tennessee Press, 1983) pertains to sixteenth-century Florida (see esp. 250–74) but is extremely flawed; see critical reviews by Jerald T. Milanich in *Agriculture and Human Values*, 2:3 (Summer 1985), 83–85, James Merrell in *Reviews in American History*, 11:3 (Sept. 1984), 354–58, and David Henige in *Journal of Interdisciplinary History*, 16:4 (Spring 1986), 701–20. Dobyns has written a useful review essay on "Disease Transfer at Contact" in *Annual Review of Anthropology*, 22 (1993), 273–91.

55. *De Soto Chronicles*, 1:83 (Gentleman from Elvas), 2:285, 298, 306 (Garcilaso de la Vega). Chester B. DePratter has argued that the epidemic may never have occurred. Hudson and Tesser, eds., *Forgotten Centuries*, 197–226 at 215–17. Russell Thornton, Jonathan Warren, and Tim Miller have suggested that the "buffer zones between the chiefdoms of the Southeast may have acted as reservoirs of smallpox, slowing, but not necessarily eliminating the spread of the disease from one chiefdom to another." Verano and Ubelaker, eds., *Disease and Demography in the Americas*, 193.

56. Mitchem and Hutchinson, *Interim Report on the Tatham Mound*, 45–46, 80.

57. Marvin T. Smith, *Archaeology of Aboriginal Culture Change in the Interior Southeast: Depopulation During the Early Historic Period*, Ripley P. Bullen Monographs in Anthropology and History, No. 6 (Gainesville: University of Florida Press and Florida State Museum, 1987); Smith, "Aboriginal Depopulation in the Postcontact Southeast," in Hudson and Tesser, eds., *Forgotten Centuries*, 257–75; Smith, "Aboriginal Population Movements in the Early Historic Period Interior Southeast," in Peter H. Wood, Gregory A. Waselkov, and M. Thomas Hatley, eds., *Powhatan's Mantle: Indians in the Colonial Southeast* (Lincoln: University of Nebraska Press, 1989), 21–34; Patricia Galloway, *Choctaw Genesis, 1500–1700* (Lincoln:

University of Nebraska Press, 1995), ch. 4. Some of the chiefdoms were devolving for ecological, demographic, and/or indigenously political reasons. See David G. Anderson, *The Savannah River Chiefdoms: Political Change in the Late Prehistoric Southeast* (Tuscaloosa: University of Alabama Press, 1994); John F. Scarry, ed., *Political Structure and Change in the Prehistoric Southeastern United States,* Ripley P. Bullen Series, Florida Museum of Natural History (Gainesville: University Press of Florida, 1996).

58. Milanich, *Florida Indians and Invasion;* Milanich and Samuel Proctor, eds., *Tacachale: Essays on the Indians of Florida and Southeastern Georgia During the Historic Period,* Ripley P. Bullen Monographs in Anthropology and History, No. 1 (Gainesville: University Presses of Florida, 1978).

59. *De Soto Chronicles,* 1:111 (Gentleman from Elvas).

II. THE WIDENING STAIN

1. The text of Philip's 1573 "Ordinances for New Discoveries" can be found in translation in John H. Parry and Robert G. Keith, eds., *New Iberian World: A Documentary History of the Discovery and Settlement of Latin America to the Early 17th Century,* 5 vols. (New York: Times Books and Hector & Rose, 1984), 1:366–71.

2. David Hurst Thomas, "The Spanish Missions of La Florida: An Overview," in Thomas, ed., *Columbian Consequences, Vol. 2: Archaeological and Historical Perspectives on the Spanish Borderlands East* (Washington, D.C.: Smithsonian Institution Press, 1990), 372–73. See also Rubén Vargas Ugarte, ed., "The First Jesuit Mission in Florida," trans. Aloysius J. Owen, [U.S. Catholic Historical Society] *Historical Records and Studies,* 25 (1935), 59–148; Félix Zubillaga, *La Florida: la misión Jesuítica (1566–1572) y la colonización española,* Bibliotheca Instituti Historici S.I., vol. 1 (Rome: Institutum Historicum S.I., 1941); Frank Marotti, Jr., "Juan Baptista de Segura and the Failure of the Florida Jesuit Mission, 1566–1572," *Florida Historical Quarterly,* 63 (Jan. 1985), 267–79.

3. Maynard Geiger, *The Franciscan Conquest of Florida (1573–1618),* Studies in Hispanic-American History, vol. 1 (Washington, D.C.: Catholic University of America, 1937), 90. Since this speech comes to us from Spanish informants at second hand, the words may not be exact but the sense is probably accurate.

4. Amy Turner Bushnell, *Situado and Sabana: Spain's Support System for the Presidio and Mission Provinces of Florida,* Anthropological Papers of the American Museum of Natural History, No. 74 (New York, 1994), 70–72; Bushnell, "Ruling 'the Republic of Indians' in Seventeenth-Century Florida," in Peter H. Wood, Gregory A. Waselkov, and M. Thomas Hatley,

eds., *Powhatan's Mantle: Indians in the Colonial Southeast* (Lincoln: University of Nebraska Press, 1989), 134–50.

5. Bushnell, *Situado and Sabana,* ch. 9, p. 131; Bushnell, "Ruling 'the Republic of Indians,' " 136, 138–40; Jerald T. Milanich, "Franciscan Missions and Native Peoples in Spanish Florida," in Charles Hudson and Carmen Chaves Tesser, eds., *The Forgotten Centuries: Indians and Europeans in the American South, 1521–1704* (Athens: University of Georgia Press, 1994), 276–303 at 295.

6. Bushnell, *Situado and Sabana,* 108–110; Bushnell, "Ruling 'the Republic of Indians,' " 136.

7. Jerald T. Milanich, *Florida Indians and the Invasion from Europe* (Gainesville: University Press of Florida, 1995), 179–83, 187; Milanich, "Franciscan Missions and Native Peoples," 282–84, 285, fig. 3, 289, 297.

8. Amy Turner Bushnell, "The Sacramental Imperative: Catholic Ritual and Indian Sedentism in the Provinces of Florida," in Thomas, ed., *Columbian Consequences,* 2: ch. 30, quotations on 475, 480, 486.

9. Amy Turner Bushnell, " 'That Demonic Game': The Campaign to Stop Indian Pelota Playing in Spanish Florida, 1675–1684," *The Americas,* 35:1 (1978), 1–19; John H. Hann, *Apalachee: The Land Between the Rivers,* Ripley P. Bullen Monographs in Anthropology and History, No. 7 (Gainesville: University of Florida Press and Florida State Museum, 1988), ch. 3, app. 2.

10. At most missions, interments were made in the floor of the church itself. Milanich, "Franciscan Missions and Native Peoples," 291.

11. *Ibid.,* 289–93; Milanich, *Florida Indians and Invasion,* 188–98; Hann, *Apalachee,* ch. 9; Rebecca Saunders, "Ideal and Innovation: Mission Architecture in the Southeast," in Thomas, ed., *Columbian Consequences,* 2: ch. 33; Saunders, "Architecture of the Missions Santa Maria and Santa Catalina de Amelia," in Bonnie G. McEwan, ed., *The Spanish Missions of "La Florida"* (Gainesville: University Press of Florida, 1993), ch. 2; David Hurst Thomas, *St. Catherines: An Island in Time,* Georgia History and Culture Series (Atlanta: Georgia Endowment for the Humanities, 1988), ch. 5.

12. John H. Hann, ed. and trans., "1630 Memorial of Fray Francisco Alonso de Jesus on Spanish Florida's Missions and Natives," *The Americas,* 50:1 (July 1993), 85–105 at 95.

13. Walter J. Ong, *The Presence of the Word: Some Prolegomena for Cultural and Religious History* (New Haven: Yale University Press, 1967), 40, 135. See also Ong, *Orality and Literacy: The Technologizing of the Word* (London and New York: Methuen, 1982).

14. Bushnell, "The Sacramental Imperative," 483; Bushnell, "Ruling 'the Republic of Indians,' " 137; Bushnell, *Situado and Sabana,* 105.

15. Bushnell, "The Sacramental Imperative," 483; Bushnell, *Situado and Sabana*, 96; Lucy L. Wenhold, ed. and trans., "A 17th Century Letter of Gabriel Diaz Vara Calderón, Bishop of Cuba, Describing the Indians and Indian Missions of Florida," *Smithsonian Miscellaneous Collections*, 95:16 (1936), 1–14 at 12.

16. Hann, ed., "1630 Memorial of Fray Alonso," 99, 101; Bushnell, "The Sacramental Imperative," 485; Robert Allen Matter, "Mission Life in Seventeenth-Century Florida," *Catholic Historical Review*, 67 (July 1981), 401–20 at 415; Bushnell, *Situado and Sabana*, 95.

17. Thomas, "The Spanish Missions of La Florida," 383–84; Thomas, *St. Catherines*, 35–40; Milanich, *Florida Indians and Invasion*, 195–98; Lisa M. Howshower and Milanich, "Excavations in the Fig Springs Mission Burial Area," in McEwan, ed., *The Spanish Missions of "La Florida,"* ch. 9.

18. Fray Alonso spoke in 1630 of "20 thousand souls baptized and more than 50,000 catechized among the catechumens" (Hann, ed., "1630 Memorial of Fray Alonso," 100). At mid-century the Franciscans counted 26,000 converts (Thomas, "The Spanish Missions of La Florida," 377). Bishop Calderón confirmed 13,152 Christian Indians in 1675 (Wenhold, ed., "A 17th Century Letter of Bishop Calderón," 12).

19. Bushnell, *Situado and Sabana*, 114–16, 122; Robert Allen Matter, "Economic Basis of the Seventeenth-Century Florida Missions," *Florida Historical Quarterly*, 52:1 (1973), 18–38 at 34–37; Charles W. Spellman [pseudonym of Michael V. Gannon], "The 'Golden Age' of the Florida Missions, 1632–1674," *Catholic Historical Review*, 51:3 (Oct. 1965), 354–72 at 361–62.

20. Bushnell, *Situado and Sabana*, ch. 11, pp. 138–42; Spellman, "The 'Golden Age' of the Florida Missions," 362–66; Hann, *Apalachee*, ch. 6; John H. Hann, ed. and trans., "Translation of Governor Rebolledo's 1657 Visitation of Three Florida Provinces and Related Documents," *Florida Archaeology*, 2 (1986), 81–146 at 87, 89, 103, 105.

21. Amy Turner Bushnell, "Background and Beginnings of the Deerskin Trade: Spanish Documentary Evidence" (Paper presented at the annual meeting of the American Society for Ethnohistory, Charleston, 1986); Gregory A. Waselkov, "Seventeenth-Century Trade in the Colonial Southeast," *Southeastern Archaeology*, 8:2 (Winter 1989), 117–33; Hann, ed., "Translation of Rebolledo's 1657 Visitation," 87, 92.

22. Bushnell, *Situado and Sabana*, 111. Archaeologists have discovered that the priests in the Apalachee breadbasket of Florida ate far better (especially more beef and pork) than did their brethren in Guale (who had some pork), and both ate much better than their colleagues in St. Augustine, who consumed a lot of fish and wild game. In the third quarter of the seventeenth century, cattle ranches flourished in Apalachee and

western Timucua; some herds were owned by Christian caciques. Elizabeth J. Reitz, "Evidence for Animal Use at the Missions in Spanish Florida," in McEwan, ed., *The Spanish Missions of "La Florida,"* ch. 14; Charles W. Arnade, "Cattle Raising in Spanish Florida," *Agricultural History*, 35:3 (1961), 3–11; Amy Turner Bushnell, "The Menéndez Marqués Cattle Barony at La Chua and the Determinants of Economic Expansion in Seventeenth-Century Florida," *Florida Historical Quarterly*, 56:4 (1978), 407–31; Hann, *Apalachee*, 239–40; Milanich, *Florida Indians and Invasion*, 199, 203, 207–208, 210–12. On the rich furnishings of mission churches, see John H. Hann, "Church Furnishings, Sacred Vessels and Vestments Held by the Missions of Florida: Translation of Two Inventories," *Florida Archaeology*, 2 (1986), 147–64; Hann, *Apalachee*, 212–17; Milanich, *Florida Indians and Invasion*, 192–95.

23. Bushnell, *Situado and Sabana*, ch. 10; Matter, "Economic Basis of the Florida Missions," 31–37; Hann, ed., "Translation of Rebolledo's 1657 Visitation," 87, 88, 93, 94, 96–98; Wenhold, ed., "A 17th Century Letter of Bishop Calderón," 13.

24. David J. Weber, *The Spanish Frontier in North America* (New Haven: Yale University Press, 1992), 115.

25. Bushnell, *Situado and Sabana*, 128–33 at 128; Milanich, *Florida Indians and Invasion*, 214–18, 221–22; Hann, *Apalachee*, 22–23, ch. 7; John H. Hann, "Demographic Patterns and Changes in Mid-Seventeenth Century Timucua and Apalachee," *Florida Historical Quarterly*, 64:4 (April 1986), 371–92.

26. Spellman, "The 'Golden Age' of the Florida Missions," 362; Hann, *Apalachee*, 19–20; John H. Hann, ed. and trans., "Translation of Alonso de Leturiondo's Memorial to the King of Spain [1700]," *Florida Archaeology*, 2 (1986), 162–225 at 178.

27. Bushnell, *Situado and Sabana*, 130–31; Amy Bushnell, "Patricio de Hinachuba: Defender of the Word, the Crown of the King, and the Little Children of Ivitachuco," *American Indian Culture and Research Journal*, 3:1 (July 1979), 1–21 at 6.

28. Clark Spencer Larsen, "On the Frontier of Contact: Mission Bioarchaeology in *La Florida*," in McEwan, ed., *The Spanish Missions of "La Florida,"* ch. 12; Larsen *et al.*, "Beyond Demographic Collapse: Biological Adaptation and Change in Native Populations of La Florida," in Thomas, ed., *Columbian Consequences*, 2:ch. 26; Larsen and Christopher B. Ruff, "The Stresses of Conquest in Spanish Florida: Structural Adaptation and Change Before and After Contact," in Larsen and George R. Milner, eds., *In the Wake of Contact: Biological Responses to Conquest* (New York: Wiley-Liss, 1994), ch. 3; Larsen *et al.*, "Population Decline and Extinction in La Florida," in John W. Verano and Douglas H. Ubelaker, eds., *Disease and*

Demography in the Americas (Washington, D.C.: Smithsonian Institution Press, 1992), ch. 4. The best data in these reports come from Santa Catalina de Guale on St. Catherines and Amelia Islands, Georgia. Some of the dietary deficiencies noted on the Atlantic coast may not have occurred with such frequency at the inland mission sites, where the natives seem to have retained their preference for wild game or substituted comparable domestic livestock for wild species.

29. Hann, ed., "Translation of Leturiondo's Memorial to the King," 175. Other aspects of acculturation resulting from Spanish contact are treated by Hann, *Apalachee,* ch. 11; Milanich, *Florida Indians and Invasion,* 198–212; Jerald Milanich and Samuel Proctor, eds., *Tacachale: Essays on the Indians of Florida and Southeastern Georgia During the Historic Period* (Gainesville: University Presses of Florida, 1978), 1–18, 59–140. On linguistic acculturation, see Cecil H. Brown, "Spanish Loanwords in Languages of the U.S. Southeast" (Unpublished paper, Northern Illinois University, Dept. of Anthropology, 1994), and William C. Sturtevant, "Spanish-Indian Relations in Southeastern North America," *Ethnohistory,* 9:1 (Winter 1962), 41–94 at 50–54, esp. 51, fig. 3.

30. Verner W. Crane, *The Southern Frontier, 1670–1732* (Ann Arbor: University of Michigan Press, 1929, 1956), chs. 2, 4; J. Leitch Wright, Jr., *The Only Land They Knew: The Tragic Story of the American Indians in the Old South* (New York: Free Press, 1981), ch. 5; Charles W. Arnade, *The Seige of St. Augustine in 1702,* University of Florida Monographs, Social Sciences, No. 3, Summer 1959 (Gainesville: University of Florida Press, 1959).

31. Hann, *Apalachee,* chs. 11–13; Milanich, *Florida Indians and Invasion,* 222–31; Mark F. Boyd, Hale G. Smith, and John W. Griffin, *Here They Once Stood: The Tragic End of the Apalachee Missions* (Gainesville: University of Florida Press, 1951), 90 (1708).

32. Hann, *Apalachee,* 388.

33. *Ibid.,* 32–33, 356; Boyd, Smith, and Griffin, *Here They Once Stood,* 35; James Axtell, *The European and the Indian: Essays in the Ethnohistory of Colonial North America* (New York: Oxford University Press, 1981), 33–34, 214.

34. David B. Quinn and Alison M. Quinn, eds., *Virginia Voyages from Hakluyt* (London: Oxford University Press, 1973), 71–73.

35. *Ibid.,* 18, 26–27, 35, 40, 74 (quotation), 99, 101. See also David Beers Quinn, *Set Fair for Roanoke: Voyages and Colonies, 1584–1606* (Chapel Hill: University of North Carolina Press, 1985).

36. Peter H. Wood, "The Changing Population of the Colonial South: An Overview by Race and Region, 1685–1790," in Wood, Waselkov, and Hatley, eds., *Powhatan's Mantle,* 35–103 at 38, table 1. R. C. Simmons estimates the non-Indian population in 1700 at 58,560. All of these numbers are

"guesstimates" without firm foundation. *The American Colonies: From Settlement to Independence* (New York: David McKay Co., 1976), 76, 87.

37. Carville V. Earle, "Environment, Disease, and Mortality in Early Virginia," in Thad W. Tate and David L. Ammerman, eds., *The Chesapeake in the Seventeenth Century: Essays on Anglo-American Society* (Chapel Hill: University of North Carolina Press, 1979), 96–125; Karen Ordahl Kupperman, "Apathy and Death in Early Jamestown," *Journal of American History*, 66 (1979), 24–40.

38. J. B. Harley, "Maps, Knowledge, and Power," in Denis Cosgrove and Stephen Daniels, eds., *The Iconography of Landscape: Essays on the Symbolic Representation, Design and Use of Past Environments* (Cambridge: Cambridge University Press, 1988), ch. 14; Harley, "Deconstructing the Map," *Cartographica*, 26:2 (Summer 1989), 1–20; Harley, *Maps and the Columbian Encounter* (Milwaukee: Golda Meir Library, University of Wisconsin, 1990); Harley, "New England Cartography and the Native Americans," in Emerson W. Baker *et al.*, eds., *American Beginnings: Exploration, Culture, and Cartography in the Land of Norumbega* (Lincoln: University of Nebraska Press, 1994), ch. 13.

39. James Axtell, *The Rise and Fall of the Powhatan Empire: Indians in Seventeenth-Century Virginia*, The Foundations of America (Williamsburg: Colonial Williamsburg Foundation, 1995), 35; a fully footnoted version appears in Axtell, *After Columbus: Essays in the Ethnohistory of Colonial North America* (New York: Oxford University Press, 1988), ch. 10 at 214.

40. Helen C. Rountree and E. Randolph Turner III, "On the Fringe of the Southeast: The Powhatan Paramount Chiefdom in Virginia," in Hudson and Tesser, eds., *Forgotten Centuries*, 355–72; Rountree, *The Powhatan Indians of Virginia: Their Traditional Culture* (Norman: University of Oklahoma Press, 1989), 140–52.

41. Martin H. Quitt, "Trade and Acculturation at Jamestown, 1607–1609: The Limits of Understanding," *William and Mary Quarterly*, 3d ser. 52:2 (April 1995), 227–58; Helen C. Rountree, *Pocahontas's People: The Powhatan Indians of Virginia Through Four Centuries* (Norman: University of Oklahoma Press, 1990), chs. 1–7. In 1608, Powhatan asked the English to send him "men to build him a house, [and to] bring him a grin[d]stone, 50. swords, some peeces [guns], a cock and a hen, with copper and beads." An immobile house and heavy grindstone would have been foolish acquisitions; he was certainly not given weapons. Philip L. Barbour, ed., *The Jamestown Voyages Under the First Charter, 1606–1609*, Hakluyt Society Publications, 2nd ser. 136–37, 2 vols. (Cambridge, 1969), 2:421 (continuous pagination).

42. Judith Reynolds, "Marriage Between the English and Indians in Seventeenth Century Virginia," *Archaeological Society of Virginia*,

NOTES TO PAGES 41–42

Quarterly Bulletin, 17:2 (Dec. 1962), 19–25; David D. Smits, "'Abominable Mixture': Toward the Repudiation of Anglo-Indian Intermarriage in Seventeenth-Century Virginia," *Virginia Magazine of History and Biography,* 95:2 (April 1987), 157–92.

43. Clarence Walworth Alvord and Lee Bidgood, eds., *The First Explorations of the Trans-Allegheny Region by the Virginians, 1650–1674* (Cleveland: The Arthur H. Clark Co., 1912); Alan Vance Briceland, *Westward from Virginia: The Exploration of the Virginia-Carolina Frontier, 1650–1710* (Charlottesville: University Press of Virginia, 1987); Mary Miley Theobald, "The Indian Trade in Colonial Virginia, 1584–1725" (M.A. thesis, Dept. of History, College of William and Mary, 1980); W. Neil Franklin, "Virginia and the Cherokee Indian Trade, 1673–1752," *East Tennessee Historical Society's Publications,* 4 (Jan. 1932), 3–21.

44. Wilcomb E. Washburn, *The Governor and the Rebel: A History of Bacon's Rebellion in Virginia* (Chapel Hill: University of North Carolina Press for the Institute of Early American History and Culture, 1957), ch. 3; H. Trawick Ward and R. P. Stephen Davis, Jr., eds., "Archaeology of the Historic Occaneechi Indians," *Southern Indian Studies,* 36–37 (Oct. 1988), 1–128.

45. William P. Cumming, ed., *The Discoveries of John Lederer* (Charlottesville: University of Virginia Press and Winston-Salem: Wachovia Historical Society, 1958), 41; Roy S. Dickens, Jr., H. Trawick Ward, and R. P. Stephen Davis, Jr., eds., *The Siouan Project: Seasons I and II,* Research Laboratories of Anthropology, University of North Carolina, Monograph Series, No. 1 (Chapel Hill, 1987), esp. ch. 2; James H. Merrell, "'Our Bond of Peace': Patterns of Intercultural Exchange in the Carolina Piedmont, 1650–1750," in Wood, Waselkov, and Hatley, eds., *Powhatan's Mantle,* 196–222; Ward and Davis, "The Impact of Old World Diseases on the Native Inhabitants of the North Carolina Piedmont," *Archaeology of Eastern North America,* 19 (1991), 171–81; Davis and Ward, "The Evolution of Siouan Communities in Piedmont North Carolina," *Southeastern Archaeology,* 10:1 (1991), 40–53.

46. Wright, *The Only Land They Knew,* ch. 5; Robert W. Weir, *Colonial South Carolina: A History,* A History of the Thirteen Colonies (Millwood, N.Y.: KTO Press, 1983), ch. 4; M. Eugene Sirmans, *Colonial South Carolina: A Political History, 1663–1763* (Chapel Hill: University of North Carolina Press for the Institute of Early American History and Culture, 1966), chs. 1–4.

47. William Owen to Lord Ashley, Sept. 15, 1670, in *Collections of the South Carolina Historical Society,* 5 (1897), 196–202 at 200–201; Alexander S. Salley, Jr., ed., *Narratives of Early Carolina, 1650–1708,* Original Narratives of Early American History (New York: Charles Scribner's Sons, 1911), 133

(Henry Woodward, 1674, punctuation added), 182–83; Crane, *The Southern Frontier,* 33–37.

48. Philip M. Brown, "Early Indian Trade in the Development of South Carolina: Politics, Economics, and Social Mobility During the Proprietary Period, 1670–1719," *South Carolina Historical Magazine,* 76 (1975), 118–28; Eirlys Barker, "Much Blood and Treasure: South Carolina's Indian Traders, 1670–1755" (Ph.D. diss., Dept. of History, College of William and Mary, 1993), ch. 3; Converse D. Clowse, *Economic Beginnings in Colonial South Carolina, 1670–1730,* Tricentennial Studies, No. 3 (Columbia: University of South Carolina Press, 1971).

49. Crane, *The Southern Frontier,* 111 (quotation), 118; Salley, ed., *Narratives of Early Carolina,* 150 (quotation), 170, 182, 289, 292 (Archdale, 1707); Vernon J. Knight, Jr., and Sherée L. Adams, "A Voyage to the Mobile and Tomeh in 1700: With Notes on the Interior of Alabama," *Ethnohistory,* 28:2 (Spring 1981), 179–94 at 182.

50. Knight and Adams, "A Voyage to the Mobile and Tomeh," 182; [Thomas] *Nairne's Muskhogean Journals: The 1708 Expedition to the Mississippi River,* ed. Alexander Moore (Jackson: University Press of Mississippi, 1988), 47; Crane, *The Southern Frontier,* 113 and n. 20; William Robert Snell, "Indian Slavery in Colonial South Carolina, 1671–1795" (Ph.D. diss., Dept. of History, University of Alabama, 1972), app. 4 (pp. 143–49).

51. Wright, *The Only Land They Knew,* 120, 122, 139, 144; Amy Ellen Friedlander, "Indian Slavery in Proprietary South Carolina" (M.A. thesis, Dept. of History, Emory University, 1975), 37–38, 49 (Dr. Francis Le Jau); W. N. Sainsbury *et al.,* eds., *Calendar of State Papers, Colonial Series: America and West Indies* (London, 1860–), 11:508–10 at 509 (Lords Proprietor, 1683); *Journal of the Commissioners for Trade and Plantations . . . ,* 14 vols. (London, 1920–1938), 3:54 (William Byrd II, 1715); *Nairne's Muskhogean Journals,* 76.

52. Wright, *The Only Land They Knew,* ch. 8; Frank J. Klingberg, "The Indian Frontier in South Carolina as Seen by the S.P.G. Missionary," *Journal of Southern History,* 5:4 (Nov. 1939), 478–500; Klingberg, ed., *The Carolina Chronicle of Dr. Francis Le Jau, 1706–1717,* University of California Publications in History, 53 (Berkeley and Los Angeles: University of California Press, 1956).

53. Friedlander, "Indian Slavery in Proprietary South Carolina," 48 (Le Jau).

III. MAKING DO

1. Wilbur R. Jacobs, ed., *The Appalachian Indian Frontier: The Edmond Atkin Report and Plan of 1755* (Columbia: University of South

Carolina Press, 1954; Lincoln: University of Nebraska Press, 1967), 3–4 (hereafter cited as *Atkin Report*).

2. *Atkin Report*, 38.

3. Dunbar Rowland, A. G. Sanders, and Patricia Kay Galloway, ed. and trans., *Mississippi Provincial Archives: French Dominion, 1701–1763*, 5 vols. (Jackson: Mississippi Department of Archives and History, and Baton Rouge: Louisiana State University Press, 1927–1984), 3:234, Bienville to Maurepas, August 26, 1734 (hereafter cited as *MPAFD*).

4. *Atkin Report*, 39.

5. [James Glen,] *A Description of South Carolina* (London, 1761), 59, 63, facsimile reprint in Chapman J. Milling, ed., *Colonial South Carolina: Two Contemporary Descriptions* (Columbia: University of South Carolina Press, 1951), 67, 71.

6. John W. Caughey, *McGillivray of the Creeks* (Norman: University of Oklahoma Press, 1938), 65.

7. [Thomas] *Nairne's Muskhogean Journals: The 1708 Expedition to the Mississippi River*, ed. Alexander Moore (Jackson: University Press of Mississippi, 1988), 56, 75.

8. *Atkin Report*, 13, 39; Journal of the [South Carolina] Commons House of Assembly, March 24, 1736, quoted in John Phillip Reid, *A Better Kind of Hatchet: Law, Trade, and Diplomacy in the Cherokee Nation During the Early Years of European Contact* (University Park: Penn State University Press, 1976), 149; John Stuart, Report to the Lord Commissioners of Trade and Plantations, March 9, 1764, quoted in Kathryn E. Holland Braund, *Deerskins & Duffels: The Creek Indian Trade with Anglo-America, 1685–1815* (Lincoln: University of Nebraska Press, 1993), 26.

9. George Croghan, 1749, quoted in Gregory A. Waselkov, "French Colonial Trade in the Upper Creek Country," in John A. Walthall and Thomas E. Emerson, eds., *Calumet & Fleur-de-Lys: Archaeology of Indian and French Contact in the Midcontinent* (Washington, D.C.: Smithsonian Institution Press, 1992), 35.

10. *MPAFD*, 3:670–71, Bienville to Maurepas, April 20, 1734.

11. Peter H. Wood, "The Changing Population of the Colonial South: An Overview by Race and Region, 1685–1790," in Wood, Gregory A. Waselkov, and M. Thomas Hatley, eds., *Powhatan's Mantle: Indians in the Colonial Southeast* (Lincoln: University of Nebraska Press, 1989), 35–103, esp. tables 1 (pp. 38–39) and 3 (p. 90).

12. *Ibid.*, 90, table 3. I have excluded Wood's figures for East Texas in each case because that region was not settled by Europeans early in the eighteenth century nor was it heavily involved in trade with the rest of the colonial Southeast.

13. Braund, *Deerskins & Duffels*, 88.

14. *Ibid.*, 68–69, 88–89.

15. Verner W. Crane, *The Southern Frontier, 1670–1732* (Ann Arbor: University of Michigan Press, 1956 [1929]), ch. 8; Reid, *A Better Kind of Hatchet,* chs. 13–15.

16. Eirlys Mair Barker, "'Much Blood and Treasure': South Carolina's Indian Traders, 1670–1755" (Ph.D. diss., College of William and Mary, Dept. of History, 1993); Braund, *Deerskins & Duffels,* chs. 3, 5–6; Reid, *A Better Kind of Hatchet,* chs. 9, 12, 15.

17. [James] *Adair's History of the American Indians* [London, 1775], ed. Samuel Cole Williams (New York: Argonaut Press, 1966), 306, 394, 444; *Atkin Report,* 36; Bernard Romans, *A Concise Natural History of East and West Florida* [facsimile of 1775 edition] (Gainesville: University of Florida Press, 1962), 60.

18. *Atkin Report,* 12, 15, 17, 23, 25.

19. Reid, *A Better Kind of Hatchet,* 42–43, 143–44; Braund, *Deerskins & Duffels,* 191; William L. McDowell, Jr., ed., *Documents Relating to Indian Affairs, 1750–1765,* Colonial Records of South Carolina, Series 2, 2 vols. (Columbia: South Carolina Department of Archives and History, 1958–70), 2:355 (hereafter cited as *S.C. Indian Records*).

20. *Atkin Report,* 35; Braund, *Deerskins & Duffels,* 89, 191, 192; Reid, *A Better Kind of Hatchet,* 170–71. A shift in European preferences in the late 1760s temporarily encouraged the importation of undressed hides.

21. *S.C. Indian Records,* 2:41–42, 334.

22. Crane, *Southern Frontier,* ch. 7, p. 167 (quotation); Reid, *A Better Kind of Hatchet,* 52–54; *S.C. Indian Records,* 2:355.

23. *S.C. Indian Records,* 2:45.

24. Braund, *Deerskins & Duffels,* 54, 148, 150–51.

25. *Calendar of State Papers, Colonial Series, America and West Indies, Preserved in the Public Record Office,* vol. 28, ed. Cecil Headlam (London: HM Stationery Office, 1928), 247–48, no. 540, Crawley to William Byrd, July 30, 1715; Braund, *Deerskins & Duffels,* 107, 192; [Dr. George Milligen-Johnston,] *A Short Description of the Province of South-Carolina* [1763] (London, 1770), 78, in Milling, ed., *Colonial South Carolina,* 188.

26. *S.C. Indian Records,* 1:283.

27. *Ibid.,* 2:267, 334; Braund, *Deerskins & Duffels,* 146, 152; Reid, *A Better Kind of Hatchet,* 137, 143, 191–92.

28. Paul Chrisler Phillips, *The Fur Trade,* 2 vols. (Norman: University of Oklahoma Press, 1961), 1:361–76, 448–51, 464–83, 536–40, 569–73; Daniel H. Usner, Jr., "The Deerskin Trade in French Louisiana," *Proceedings of the Tenth Meeting of the French Colonial Historical Society, April 12–14, 1984,* ed. Philip P. Boucher (Lanham, M.D.: University Press of America, 1985), 75–93; N. M. Miller Surrey, *The Commerce of Louisiana*

During the French Regime, 1699–1763, Columbia University Studies in the Social Sciences 167 (New York: Columbia University Press, 1916; AMS Press, 1968), ch. 19.

29. James M. Crawford, *The Mobilian Trade Language* (Knoxville: University of Tennessee Press, 1978); Ian W. Brown, "The Calumet Ceremony in the Southeast and Its Archaeological Manifestations," *American Antiquity,* 54 (1989), 311–31; *MPAFD,* 3:565–66, King to Bienville and Salmon, February 2, 1732.

30. *Atkin Report,* 9–10, 63. The cost to the crown of presents was not inconsiderable. In 1713, Indian presents had cost only 4,000 livres; by 1744, they had exploded to 73,617 livres (*MPAFD,* 2:147; Phillips, *The Fur Trade,* 1:473). See *MPAFD,* 5:228–30 for a list of presents ordered in 1758–59.

31. *Atkin Report,* 10–11, 29; *MPAFD,* 1:193, 2:249–50, 4:46, 159n.8; Gregory A. Waselkov, Brian M. Wood, and Joseph M. Herbert, *Colonization and Conquest: The 1980 Archaeological Excavations at Fort Toulouse and Fort Jackson, Alabama,* Auburn University Archaeological Monograph 4 (Montgomery, Ala., 1982), 93–99.

32. *Atkin Report,* 6, 12, 15, 17, 23, 25.

33. *Ibid.,* 12–13; *MPAFD,* 3:515.

34. Joseph and Nesta Ewan, *John Banister and His Natural History of Virginia, 1678–1692* (Urbana: University of Illinois Press, 1970), 41–42; *Travels of William Bartram,* ed. Mark Van Doren (New York: Dover, 1955), 184, 401.

35. James Axtell, "At the Water's Edge: Trading in the Sixteenth Century," *After Columbus: Essays in the Ethnohistory of Colonial North America* (New York: Oxford University Press, 1988), ch. 9.

36. *MPAFD,* 5:228–32 (1758–59). In 1731, Choctaws suffering from disease blamed English traders for planting bad medicine made from sugar cane in the limbourg they traded to the Choctaws via the Chickasaws (*MPAFD,* 4:58–59, Régis du Roullet to Périer, February 21, 1731).

37. *S.C. Indian Records,* 2:423 (December 26, 1757).

38. Braund, *Deerskins & Duffels,* 123.

39. *Nairne's Muskhogean Journals,* 57.

40. Braund, *Deerskins & Duffels,* illus. 1, 6–7, 9–12 (following p. 108); *Von Reck's Voyage: Drawings and Journals of Philip Georg Friedrich von Reck,* ed. Kristian Hvidt (Savannah: Beehive Press, 1980), 107, 111, 115, 118, 127, 129.

41. Braund, *Deerskins & Duffels,* illus. 1, 6–7, 9, 11; *Von Reck's Voyage,* 117, 119, 127.

42. *MPAFD,* 5:228–32; [William Gerard] *De Brahm's Report of the General Survey in the Southern District of North America* [1765–66], ed. Louis

90

DeVorsey, Jr., Tricentennial Edition, No. 3 (Columbia: University of South Carolina Press, 1971), 107; *S.C. Indian Records*, 2:567–68, 576–79.

43. James Axtell, "The First Consumer Revolution," *Beyond 1492: Encounters in Colonial North America* (New York: Oxford University Press, 1992), ch. 5.

44. Dorothy Downs, "British Influences on Creek and Seminole Men's Clothing, 1733–1858," *Florida Anthropologist*, 33 (1980), 46–65; Braund, *Deerskins & Duffels*, 124–25.

45. Jeffrey P. Brain, *Tunica Treasure*, Papers of the Peabody Museum of Archaeology and Ethnology 71 (Cambridge, Mass.: Harvard University, and Salem, Mass.: Peabody Museum of Salem, 1979); Brain, *Tunica Archaeology*, Papers of the Peabody Mus. of Arch. and Ethnol. 78 (Cambridge, Mass.: Harvard University, 1988), 327. The Creeks around Fort Toulouse made traditional pottery and colono ware for the use of the French soldiers and settlers there (Waselkov, "French Colonial Trade in the Upper Creek Country," 44). On the Creek preference for their own pottery, see Carol Mason, "Eighteenth Century Culture Change Among the Lower Creeks," *Florida Anthropologist*, 16 (September 1963), 65–80 at 69.

46. *MPAFD*, 1:349 (1737). See also *MPAFD*, 2:613; *De Brahm's Report*, 107, "Guns (very slight)."

47. *MPAFD*, 5:228–32.

48. *Atkin Report*, 11, 12, 52, 57–58 (quotation), 64. See also Newton D. Mereness, ed., *Travels in the American Colonies* (New York: Antiquarian Press, 1961), 290 (De Beauchamps, 1746); *MPAFD*, 4:209.

49. Mereness, ed., *Travels in the American Colonies*, 250 (Antoine Bonnefoy, 1741–42); *MPAFD*, 5:232.

50. David H. Corkran, *The Cherokee Frontier: Conflict and Survival, 1740–62* (Norman: University of Oklahoma Press, 1962), 69 (1756); *S.C. Indian Records*, 2:296; Braund, *Deerskins & Duffels*, 122, 190.

51. *MPAFD*, 5:229–31; *Jean-Bernard Bossu's Travels in the Interior of North America, 1751–1762*, ed. and trans. Seymour Feiler (Norman: University of Oklahoma Press, 1962), 116; *Von Reck's Voyage*, 47–48.

52. *Adair's History*, 245; M. Le Page du Pratz, *The History of Louisiana* [Paris, 1758] (London, 1774), ed. Joseph G. Tregle, Jr., Louisiana Bicentennial Reprint Series (Baton Rouge: Louisiana State University Press, 1975), 305–306. On the psychological importance of mirrors, see Michelle Perrot, ed., *A History of Private Life. Vol. 4: From the Fires of Revolution to the Great War*, trans. Arthur Goldhammer (Cambridge, Mass.: Harvard University Press, 1990), 460 (Alain Corbin); James W. Fernandez, "Reflections on Looking into Mirrors," *Semiotica*, 30:1–2 (1980), 27–39; Benjamin Goldberg, *The Mirror and Man* (Charlottesville: University Press of Virginia, 1985).

53. John Lawson, *A New Voyage to Carolina* [London, 1709], ed. Hugh Talmage Lefler (Chapel Hill: University of North Carolina Press, 1967), 210, 212, 232; Braund, *Deerskins & Duffels*, 125–27, 146; John Brickell, *The Natural History of North-Carolina* [Dublin, 1737] (New York: Johnson Reprint Corporation, 1969), 292–93; *De Brahm's Report*, 108; W. L. McDowell, ed., *Journals of the Commissioners of the Indian Trade, September 20, 1710–August 29, 1718*, Col. Recs. of S.C., Ser. 2 (Columbia: S.C. Archives Dept., 1955), 104. On native prohibition efforts, see Peter C. Mancall, *Deadly Medicine: Indians and Alcohol in Early America* (Ithaca: Cornell University Press, 1995), ch. 5. Archaeologists have found liquor bottles on many Indian sites. See, for example, Brain, *Tunica Treasure*, 85–93; George I. Quimby, *The Bayou Goula Site, Iberville Parish, Louisiana*, Fieldiana: Anthropology, 47:2 (Chicago: Chicago Natural History Museum, 1957), 135–36; Vernon James Knight, Jr., *Tukabatchee: Archaeological Investigations at an Historic Creek Town, Elmore County, Alabama, 1984*, Report of Investigations 45, Office of Archaeological Research, Alabama State Museum of Natural History, University of Alabama (Tuscaloosa, 1985), 123, 126; Kurt C. Russ and Jefferson Chapman, *Archaeological Investigations at the Eighteenth Century Overhill Cherokee Town of Mialoquo (40MR3)*, Report of Investigations, No. 37, Dept. of Anthropology, University of Tennessee, and Tennessee Valley Authority Publications in Anthropology, No. 36 (Knoxville, 1983), 100, 102; Gerald F. Schroedl, ed., *Overhill Cherokee Archaeology at Chota-Tanasee*, Report of Investigations, No. 38, Dept. of Anthrop., U. of Tenn., and TVA Pubs. in Anthrop., No. 42 (Knoxville, 1986), 418–19.

54. Lawson, *New Voyage to Carolina*, 232–33; *Travels of William Bartram*, 214–15.

55. *Von Reck's Voyage*, 48–49; *Travels of William Bartram*, 399; Louis Le Clerc de Milford, *Memoir; or, A Cursory Glance at My Different Travels & My Sojourn in the Creek Nation*, ed. John Francis McDermott, trans. Geraldine de Courcy (Chicago: R. R. Donnelley and Sons, 1956), 152.

56. *Lieut. Henry Timberlake's Memoirs, 1756–1765*, ed. Samuel Cole Williams (Johnson City, Tenn.: Watauga Press, 1927), 90–91; *Adair's History*, 187; Braund, *Deerskins & Duffels*, 130; Alexander Longe, "A Small Postscript of the Ways and Manners of the Indians called Cherokees [1725]," ed. David H. Corkran, *Southern Indian Studies*, 21 (October 1969), 3–49 at 26.

57. Brain, *Tunica Archaeology*, 327 (kettles); *De Brahm's Report*, 109 (tattoos); *Adair's History*, 7; Schroedl, *Chota-Tanasee*, 441, fig. 8.11.h, 444 (hair pluckers).

58. Brain, *Tunica Archaeology*, 192, fig. 156k, l; Knight, *Tukabatchee*, 134–35, pl. 5.5c; Schroedl, *Chota-Tanasee*, 441, fig. 8.11.a–b (kettles);

Richebourg Gaillard McWilliams, ed. and trans., *Fleur de Lys and Calumet: Being the Pénicaut Narrative of French Adventure in Louisiana* (Baton Rouge: Louisiana State University Press, 1953), 99–100; Schroedl, *Chota Tanasee,* 443, fig. 8.12.d (gun barrels); Brain, *Tunica Treasure,* 186, 196 (skimmer); Schroedl, *Chota-Tanasee,* 442 (gorget); Brain, *Tunica Archaeology,* 193, fig. 156w; Lawson, *New Voyage to Carolina,* 63; Robert S. Neitzel, *The Grand Village of the Natchez Revisited: Excavations at the Fatherland Site, Adams County, Mississippi, 1972,* Archaeological Report, No. 12, Miss. Dept. of Archives and History (Jackson, 1983), pl. xxix.f (bottle glass); Brain, *Tunica Archaeology,* 100, fig. 78l, m; Russ and Chapman, *Mialoquo,* 125 (gun flints); William W. Baden, *Tomotley: An Eighteenth Century Cherokee Village,* Report of Investigations, No. 36, Dept. of Anthrop., U. of Tenn., and TVA Pubs. in Anthrop., No. 35 (Knoxville, 1983), 185, fig. II.4.d, 196 (candleholder), 186, fig. II.5.f, 194; Schroedl, *Chota-Tanasee,* 425 (bale seals).

59. Charles Hudson, *The Southeastern Indians* (Knoxville: University of Tennessee Press, 1976), 327–36; James Axtell, "Last Rights: The Acculturation of Native Funerals in Colonial North America," *The European and the Indian: Essays in the Ethnohistory of Colonial North America* (New York: Oxford University Press, 1981), ch. 5.

60. *S.C. Indian Records,* 2:152 (July 31, 1756).

61. Braund, *Deerskins & Duffels,* 75, 192 (John Stuart, Creek treaty, 1767); *S.C. Indian Records,* 2:357.

62. Braund, *Deerskins & Duffels,* 72, 75–76; *Adair's History,* 138, 242; *De Brahm's Report,* 122; Robert D. Newman, "The Acceptance of European Domestic Animals by the 18th Century Cherokee," *Tennessee Anthropologist,* 4:1 (1979), 101–107.

63. *Adair's History,* 139–40, 241, 242; *S.C. Indian Records,* 2:264 (December 8, 1756).

64. *Adair's History,* 139, 242; Braund, *Deerskins & Duffels,* 67, 76–77; Schroedl, *Chota-Tanasee,* 481; James Taylor Carson, "Horses and the Economy and Culture of the Choctaw Indians, 1690–1840," *Ethnohistory,* 42:3 (Summer 1995), 495–513.

65. *De Brahm's Report,* 110–111n.; [Mark] *Catesby's Birds of Colonial America* [London, 1731–43], ed. Alan Feduccia, Fred W. Morrison Series in Southern Studies (Chapel Hill: University of North Carolina Press, 1985), 147; Charles M. Hudson, Jr., "Why the Southeastern Indians Slaughtered Deer," in Shepard Krech III, ed., *Indians, Animals, and the Fur Trade: A Critique of "Keepers of the Game"* (Athens: University of Georgia Press, 1981), ch. 7.

66. George R. Milner, "Epidemic Disease in the Postcontact Southeast: A Reappraisal," *Mid-Continental Journal of Archaeology,* 5:1 (1980), 39–56; Ann F.

Ramenofsky, *Vectors of Death: The Archaeology of European Contact* (Albuquerque: University of New Mexico Press, 1987); Peter H. Wood, "The Impact of Smallpox on the Native Population of the 18th Century South," *New York State Journal of Medicine,* 87 (January 1987), 30–36; Calvin Martin, "Wildlife Diseases as a Factor in the Depopulation of the North American Indian," *Western Historical Quarterly,* 7:1 (January 1976), 47–62.

67. Ian K. Steele, *Warpaths: Invasions of North America* (New York: Oxford University Press, 1994), chs. 2–3, 7–8; James Axtell, "Scalping: The Ethnohistory of a Moral Question," *The European and the Indian,* ch. 8; Almon Wheeler Lauber, *Indian Slavery in Colonial Times Within the Present Limits of the United States* (Williamstown, Mass.: Corner House, 1979 [1913]); William Robert Snell, "Indian Slavery in Colonial South Carolina, 1671–1795" (Ph.D. diss., University of Alabama, Dept. of History, 1972); *Nairne's Muskhogean Journals,* 38, 41 (war chiefs).

68. Jack D. Forbes, *Africans and Native Americans: The Language of Race and the Evolution of Red-Black Peoples* (2d ed., Urbana and Chicago: University of Illinois Press, 1993); Alexander Spoehr, *Changing Kinship Systems: A Study in the Acculturation of the Creeks, Cherokee, and Choctaw,* Anthropological Series 33:4, Field Museum of Natural History (Chicago, 1947); Alan Gallay, "Indian-Black Relations on the Southern Colonial Frontier" (Paper presented at the annual meeting of the Organization of American Historians, Washington, D.C., March 1990); Kenneth Wiggins Porter, *The Negro on the American Frontier* (New York: Arno Press, 1971), 7–137, 154–81; Theda Perdue, *Slavery and the Evolution of Cherokee Society, 1540–1866* (Knoxville: University of Tennessee Press, 1979); Eirlys Barker, "Networking in the Colonial Southeast: Indian Traders and Carolina Customers" (Paper presented at the Colloquium on Indians of the Americas, College of William and Mary, February 1996); Braund, *Deerskins & Duffels,* 78, 83–85, 107–108.

69. Theda Perdue, "Cherokee Women: A Study in Changing Gender Roles" (Paper presented at the annual meeting of the American Historical Association, San Francisco, December 1989); Raymond D. Fogelson, "On the 'Petticoat Government' of the Eighteenth-Century Cherokee," in David K. Jordan and Marc J. Swartz, eds., *Personality and the Cultural Construction of Society* (Tuscaloosa: University of Alabama Press, 1990), 161–81; Kathryn E. Holland Braund, "Guardians of Tradition and Hand-maidens to Change: Women's Roles in Creek Economic and Social Life during the Eighteenth Century," *American Indian Quarterly,* 14:3 (Summer 1990), 239–58; Thomas Hatley, "Cherokee Women Farmers Hold Their Ground," in Robert D. Mitchell, ed., *Appalachian Frontiers: Settlement, Society, and Development in the Preindustrial Era* (Lexington: University Press of Kentucky, 1991), 37–51, 289–93.

70. Braund, *Deerskins & Duffels*, ch. 7; *William Byrd's Histories of the Dividing Line Betwixt Virginia and North Carolina* [London, 1728], ed. William K. Boyd (New York: Dover, 1967), 116 (April 7, 1728); K. G. Davies, ed., *Documents of the American Revolution, 1770–1783*, 20 vols. (Dublin: Irish University Press, 1972–79), 8:91 (April 14, 1774); *Travels of William Bartram*, 401.

71. A. S. Salley, indexer, *Records in the British Public Record Office Relating to South Carolina, 1663–[1710]*, 5 vols. (Atlanta: Foote and Davies, and Columbia: Historical Commission of South Carolina, 1928–47), 1:116, 118 (March 7, 1680/81).

72. *S.C. Indian Records*, 1:453 (July 3, 1753).

73. Du Pratz, *History of Louisiana*, 44–45.

74. Quoted in Braund, *Deerskins & Duffels*, 26, 30.

75. Milling, ed., *Colonial South Carolina*, 185.

INDEX

INDEX

Warfare: Indian, 21, 40, 69; Spanish, 20–21, 23. *See also* Uprisings, Indian
Weapons: Indian, 62, 69; pictured, 55, 57; Spanish, 20–21, 23. *See also* Swords
Weber, David, 35
Westoe Indians, 42

Wire, 63, 67
Women. *See* Indian women; Spanish women
Wood, Peter, 47

Yamasee Indians, 42, 51
Yuchi (Creek) Indians: pictured, 58, 59, 60